Assessment Tests for
Standard Grade
Chemistry

D A Buchanan

**(Faculty of Education,
University of Edinburgh)**

J R Melrose

**(Lenzie Academy,
Lenzie, Glasgow)**

CW01426332

Published by
Chemcord
Inch Keith
East Kilbride
Glasgow

ISBN 1 870570 78 2

© Chemcord, 2002

All rights reserved. No part of this
publication may be reproduced or
transmitted in any form or by any means,
electronic or mechanical, including
photocopy, recording, or any information
storage and retrieval system, without
permission in writing from the publisher
or under licence from the Copyright
Licensing Agency.

Printed by Bell and Bain Ltd, Glasgow

Contents

Note to teachers / lecturers

The tests are specifically designed to pin-point learning difficulties and to check students' understanding of the work covered in the Standard Grade Chemistry course. The tests have been used over a number of years and found to be an invaluable aid to learning.

While the tests can be administered to the whole class, it is suggested that they can be more effectively used by students working at their own pace in class, during self-study time in school or as homework. The information from the results of the tests can be used to help students to plan revision. The test results can also be used by teachers / lecturers who are interested in assessing individual or class difficulties.

Each test is, by and large, independent of the others and consequently the tests can be used to fit almost any teaching order.

The variation in length of the tests is a reflection of the different kinds of question which are associated with a particular area of content. Consequently, different allocations of time are required.

Acknowledgement

A number of questions in the tests come from, or have evolved from, questions used in the SCE examinations. The publisher wishes to thank the Scottish Qualifications Authority for permission to use examination questions in these ways.

General level

Decide whether each of the following is

    A. a chemical reaction   **B.** **NOT** a chemical reaction.

1. mixing two solutions to produce a gas

2. mixing two solutions to form a yellow solid

3. water boiling in a kettle

4. mixing sand and water

5. blowing bubbles of air through water

6. petrol burning in a car engine

7. mixing salt and pepper

8. dissolving sugar in tea

9. breaking up a lump of chalk to make powder

10. milk being produced in a cow

11. mould forming on stale bread

12. adding milk to coffee

13. a gas explosion

14. a leaf growing on a tree

15. breaking glass

16. burning paper

17. separating a solid from a liquid

18. food digesting in the stomach

19. melting a plastic

20. making toast from bread

21. using a magnet to separate iron from a mixture

22. new skin forming over a cut

23. a pea forming in a pod

24. cutting bread

25. paint drying on a fence

Test 1.2 Elements and compounds

General level

In questions 1 to 18, decide whether each of the following substances is

A. an element **B.** a compound.

1. Na
2. H_2
3. NO
4. Fe
5. C
6. HNO_3
7. calcium sulphide
8. sodium
9. bromine
10. aluminium oxide
11. magnesium nitrate
12. iron
13. sugar
14. sulphur
15. vinegar
16. gold
17. sand
18. salt

In questions 19 to 24, decide whether each of the following lists of substances contains

A. **only** elements

B. **only** compounds

C. **both** elements and compounds.

19. copper sulphide, copper, zinc
20. nitrogen, oxygen, magnesium
21. sodium chloride, lead sulphide, carbon dioxide
22. O_2, Mg, Br_2
23. NaBr, KF, N_2
24. Zn, H_2O, H_2

Test 1.3   Names of compounds

General level

In questions 1 to 6, name the compounds formed from each of the following pairs of elements.

1. copper and chlorine
2. sodium and oxygen
3. iron and bromine
4. lead and sulphur
5. hydrogen and iodine
6. magnesium and nitrogen

In questions 7 to 18, name the elements in each of the following compounds.

7. hydrogen oxide
8. copper sulphate
9. magnesium nitride
10. sodium carbonate
11. nitrogen hydride
12. carbon chloride
13. sodium sulphide
14. calcium sulphite
15. potassium nitrate
16. aluminium bromide
17. sodium phosphate
18. potassium chromate

General level

Decide whether each of the following statements is

    A. TRUE   **B.** FALSE.

1. Increasing the temperature increases the rate of a reaction.

2. Lumps of calcium carbonate react faster than calcium carbonate powder, with acid.

3. A dilute acid reacts faster than a more concentrated acid.

4. A catalyst can speed up the rate of a reaction.

5. Milk is more likely to turn sour at 0 °C than at 10 °C.

6. Small potatoes take longer to cook than large potatoes.

7. Plants grow faster in warm weather than in cold weather.

8. Compared with coal dust, lumps of coal burn very rapidly .

9. A catalyst can be recovered chemically unchanged at the end of a reaction.

10. Catalysts can be used in car exhaust systems to speed up the reactions which remove harmful gases.

11. Methane burns less rapidly in pure oxygen than in air.

12. Chips cook faster in oil at 300 °C than in oil at 200 °C.

13. A catalyst is used up during a chemical reaction.

14. Reactions involving gases go faster when the pressure is increased.

Questions 15 to 18 refer to reactions of acids.

Each of the following graphs show data obtained from two reactions **X** and **Y**.

A.

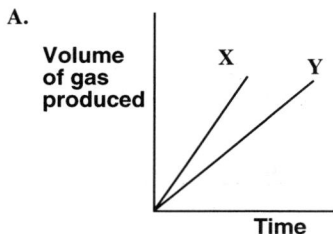

B.

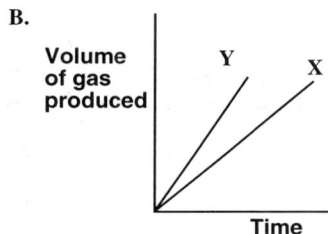

Which graph shows data which could be obtained from each of the following reactions?

(Only the variable shown is changed in each reaction.)

	Reaction **X**	Reaction **Y**
15.	chalk lumps / dilute acid	chalk powder / dilute acid
16.	metal / concentrated acid	metal / dilute acid
17.	metal / dilute acid at 10 ºC	metal / dilute acid at 30 ºC
18.	metal / dilute acid with catalyst	metal / dilute acid without catalyst

Questions 19 to 22 refer to four reactions of zinc with excess hydrochloric acid.

Curve **P** was obtained using 1 g zinc powder and 1 mol/l acid at 20 °C.

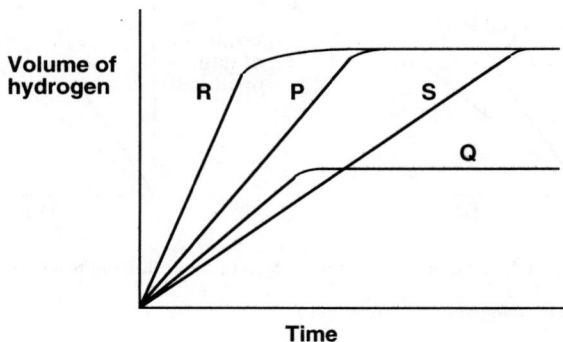

19.   Which curve could have been obtained using 1 g zinc powder and 1 mol/l acid at 10 °C.

20.   Which curve could have been obtained using 0.5 g zinc powder and 1 mol/l acid at 20 °C.

21.   Which curve could have been obtained using 1 g zinc powder and 1 mol/l acid at 30 °C.

22.   Which curve could have been obtained using 1 g zinc lumps and 1 mol/l acid at 20 °C.

General level

In questions 1 to 12, decide whether each of the following elements is

      A. a metal   **B.** a non-metal.

(You may wish to use the Data Booklet.)

1.	silver	7.	arsenic
2.	sulphur	8.	cobalt
3.	magnesium	9.	mercury
4.	iodine	10.	platinum
5.	aluminium	11.	astatine
6.	sodium	12.	rhodium

In questions 13 to 24, decide whether each of the following elements, at room temperature (20 ᵒC), is

      A.   a solid   **B.**   a liquid   **C.**   a gas.

(You may wish to use the Data Booklet.)

13.	oxygen	19.	chlorine
14.	iodine	20.	bromine
15.	phosphorus	21.	silicon
16.	hydrogen	22.	mercury
17.	calcium	23.	argon
18.	potassium	24.	fluorine

In questions 25 to 36, decide whether each of the following elements is

    A. found naturally as the element

    B. found naturally in compounds but **NOT** as the element

    C. made by scientists.

25.   gold

26.   americium

27.   calcium

28.   aluminium

29.   fermium

30.   silver

31.   magnesium

32.   sodium

33.   oxygen

34.   chlorine

35.   copper

36.   californium

General level.

1. Approximately how many elements are in the Periodic Table?

    A. 43   **B.** 73   **C.** 103   **D.** 133

2. How many elements in the Periodic Table are noble (inert) gases?

    A. 3   **B.** 6   **C.** 9   **D.** 100

3. Approximately how many metals are in the Periodic Table?

    A. 40   **B.** 60   **C.** 80   **D.** 100

4. If a new element was to be discovered this year, it would most likely be

    A. found in the sea   **B.** found in a rock

    C. made in the laboratory   **D.** found in the atmosphere.

Questions 5 to 8 refer to ways of arranging elements in the Periodic Table.

Decide whether the elements in each of the following lists are in

    A. the same group   **B.** the same period.

5. sodium, potassium, lithium

6. carbon, nitrogen, oxygen

7. phosphorus, aluminium, chlorine

8. chlorine, iodine, fluorine

Questions 9 to12 refer to chemical properties of elements.

Which element does **not** have similar chemical properties to the others?

9.	**A.**	neon	**B.**	argon	**C.**	fluorine	**D.**	xenon.
10.	**A.**	calcium	**B.**	aluminium	**C.**	strontium	**D.**	magnesium
11.	**A.**	chlorine	**B.**	astatine	**C.**	iodine	**D.**	hydrogen
12.	**A.**	caesium	**B.**	potassium	**C.**	selenium	**D.**	rubidium

In questions 13 to 18, decide whether each of the following elements is

    A. stored under oil   **B.** **NOT** stored under oil.

13.   gold

14.   sodium

15.   magnesium

16.   potassium

17.   lithium

18.   aluminium

In questions 19 to 24, decide whether each of the following elements

    A. reacts readily with other substances

    B. does **NOT** react readily with other substances.

19.   chlorine

20.   neon

21.   calcium

22.   helium

23.   argon

24.   sodium

General level

The questions in this test refer to families of elements in the Periodic Table.

    A. the halogens.

    B. the alkali metals

    C. the noble (inert) gases

    D. the transition metals

    E. none of these

Use a Periodic Table to decide the family to which each of the following elements belongs.

1.   chlorine

2.   oxygen

3.   iron

4.   argon

5.   sodium

6.   iodine

7.   magnesium

8.   neon

9.   copper

10.   potassium

11.   platinum

12.   fluorine

13.   aluminium

14.   helium

15.   rubidium

16.   mercury

17.   phosphorus

18.   zinc

19.   xenon

20.   lead

General level

1. The nucleus of an atom

    A. is positively charged

    B. is negatively charged

    C. has no charged particles

    D. has both positively and negatively charged particles.

Questions 2 and 3 refer to electrons.

2. Electrons are found

    A. in the nucleus

    B. outside the nucleus

    C. both inside and outside the nucleus.

3. Electrons are particles which

    A. have a positive charge

    B. have a negative charge

    C. have no charge

    D. can have either a positive or a negative charge.

4. An atom is neutral because

    A. the positive charge of the nucleus is equal to the sum of the negative charges of the electrons

    B. the negative charge of the nucleus is equal to the sum of the positive charges of the electrons

    C. it does not contain any charged particles.

Questions 5 to 8 refer to the following atomic numbers.

    A. 2   **B.**   11   **C.** 17   **D.**   26

What is the atomic number of each of the following elements?

5.   sodium

6.   helium

7.   chlorine

8.   iron

Questions 9 to 12 refer to the following elements.

    A.   aluminium   **B.**   carbon   **C.**   silver   **D.**   iodine

What is the element with each of the following atomic numbers?

9.   6

10.   47

11.   13

12.   53

Questions 13 to 16 refer to the following numbers of electrons.

    A.   1   **B.**   16   **C.**   29   **D.**   35

What is the number of electrons in atoms of each of the following elements?

13.   hydrogen

14.   copper

15.   sulphur

16.   bromine

Questions 17 to 20 refer to the following elements.

    A.   calcium   **B.**   silicon   **C.**   lead   **D.**   mercury

What is the element with atoms which have each of the following numbers of electrons?

17.   14

18.   80

19.   20

20.   82

Test 3.5　　　　Electron arrangement and the Periodic Table

General level

1.　Elements in the same group (column) of the Periodic Table have the same

　　A.　atomic number

　　B.　number of electrons

　　C.　number of energy levels (shells)

　　D.　number of outer electrons.

Questions 2 to 5 refer to the electron arrangements shown below.

　　A.　2,4　　　　　B.　2,8,8,2　　　　C.　2,1　　　　D.　2,8

What is the electron arrangement in an atom of each of the following elements?

2.　calcium

3.　carbon

4.　neon

5.　lithium

Questions 6 to 9 refer to the following electron arrangements.

　　A.　2,8,8　　　　B.　2,8,1　　　　C.　2,8,6　　　　D.　2,2

What is the electron arrangement in an atom with each of the following atomic numbers?

6.　11

7.　18

8.　4

9.　16

Questions 10 to 13 refer to the following numbers of outer electrons.

　　A.　2　　　　　B.　8　　　　　C.　4　　　　　D.　7

What is the number of outer electrons in an atom of each of the following elements?

10.　argon

11.　silicon

12.　magnesium

13.　chlorine

Questions 14 to 17 refer to the following numbers of outer electrons.

    A. 6   **B.** 3   **C.** 1   **D.** 5

What is the number of outer electrons in an atom with each of the following atomic numbers?

14.   8

15.   7

16.   3

17.   13

Questions 18 to 21 refer to the following elements.

    A. chlorine   **B.** lithium   **C.** magnesium   **D.** helium

Which element has similar chemical properties to each of the following atoms?

18.   an atom with an electron arrangement of 2,8,1

19.   an atom with an electron arrangement of 2,8

20.   an atom with an atomic number of 9

21.   an atom with an atomic number of 20

Question 22 to 25 refer to the electron arrangements shown below.

    A. 2,8,7   **B.** 2,8,8,2   **C .** 2,8   **D.** 2,8,1

Which is the electron arrangement in an atom with similar chemical properties to each of the following atoms?

22.   an atom with an electron arrangement 2,8,8,1

23.   an atom with an electron arrangement 2,7

24.   an atom with an atomic number 18

25.   an atom with an atomic number 4

Credit level

Questions 1 to 5 refer to the atomic particles.

    A.   proton   **B.**   neutron   **C.**   electron

1.   Which particle has a positive charge ?

2.   Which particle has a negative charge?

3.   Which particle is neutral?

4.   Which particle does **not** have a mass of 1 amu?

5.   Which particle will pass through an electric field without being deflected?

Questions 6 and 7 refer to pairs of atomic particles.

    A. neutrons and electrons

    B. neutrons and protons

    C. protons and electrons

6.   What two particles are found in the nucleus?

7.   What two particles are almost totally responsible for the mass of an atom?

8.   An atom is neutral because it contains

    A.   a number of electrons equal to the sum of the numbers of protons and neutrons

    B.   a number of neutrons equal to the sum of the numbers of electrons and protons

    C.   a number of protons equal to the number of neutrons

    D.   a number of electrons equal to the number of protons.

9.   An atom is made up of 6 protons, 6 electrons and 8 neutrons.

     It will have a mass approximately equal to that of

    A.   6 protons   **B.**   12 protons

    C.   8 protons   **D.**   14 protons.

10.   An atom is made up of 17 protons, 17 electrons and 18 neutrons.

     It will have a mass approximately equal to that of

    A.   17 neutrons   **B.**   34 neutrons

    C.   18 neutrons   **D.**   35 neutrons.

Questions 11 and 12 refer to Rutherford's experiment in which fast moving positive particles were projected at atoms of thin gold foil as shown. This experiment led to our present model of the atom.

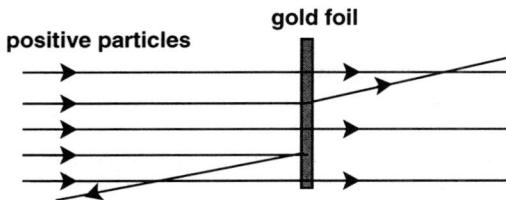

gold foil

positive particles

11.   Which of the following best explains why some of the particles are deflected?

   A.   They bounce off the surface of the foil.

   B.   They are attracted by other positive particles.

   C.   They are deflected by the electrons in the atoms of gold.

   D.   They are deflected by the atomic nuclei in the gold.

12.   The diagrams show the angle of scatter for three particles.

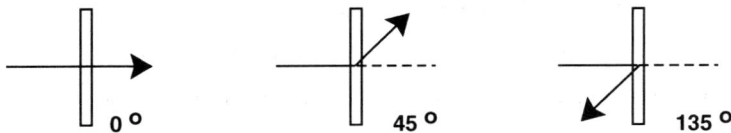

Which of the following graphs would represent the results from Rutherford's experiment?

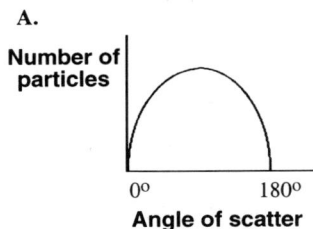

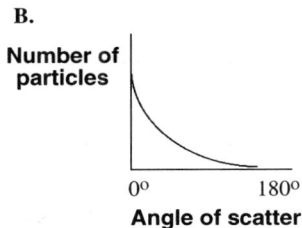

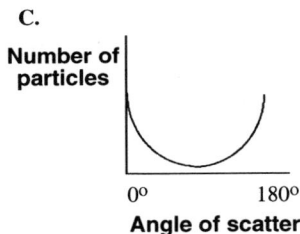

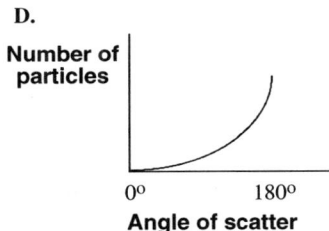

A.

Number of particles

0°   180°
Angle of scatter

B.

Number of particles

0°   180°
Angle of scatter

C.

Number of particles

0°   180°
Angle of scatter

D.

Number of particles

0°   180°
Angle of scatter

Atoms and the Periodic Table   17

Credit level

1. All atoms of the one element must have the same

   A. mass number **B.** number of neutrons

   C. atomic number **D.** number of particles in the nucleus.

2. The number of protons in an atom is equal to the

   A. mass number **B.** number of neutrons

   C. number of electrons **D.** mass number less atomic number.

3. The atomic number of an atom gives the number of

   A. neutrons **B.** protons

   C. protons and neutrons **D.** electrons and neutrons.

4. The number of neutrons in an atom is equal to the

   A. number of protons **B.** number of electrons

   C. mass number less atomic number **D.** atomic number less mass number.

5. The mass number of an atom is calculated by adding together the number of

   A. protons and electrons **B.** protons and neutrons

   C. neutrons and electrons **D.** protons, neutrons and electrons.

6. The number of electrons in an atom is equal to the

   A. atomic number **B.** mass number

   C. number of neutrons **D.** mass number less atomic number.

7. An atom of an element has 10 electrons, 12 neutrons and 10 protons.

   What is its mass number?

   A. 12 **B.** 20 **C.** 22 **D.** 32

8. An atom of an element has 92 protons and 151 neutrons.

   What is its atomic number?

   A. 59 **B.** 92 **C.** 151 **D.** 243

9. The number of electrons in an atom is 34 and the mass number is 79.

    What is the number of neutrons in the atom?

    A.   11   **B.**   34   **C.**   45   **D.**   79

10. An atom has 26 protons, 26 electrons and 30 neutrons.

    The atom will have

    A.   atomic number 26, mass number 56

    B.   atomic number 56, mass number 30

    C.   atomic number 30, mass number 26

    D.   atomic number 52, mass number 56.

11. An atom has atomic number 20 and mass number of 40.

    The nucleus of this atom contains:

	Protons	**Neutrons**
A.	10	10
B.	20	20
C.	20	40
D.	40	40

12. An atom has atomic number 23 and mass number 51.

    What is the number of electrons in the atom?

    A.   23   **B.**   28   **C.**   51   **D.**   74

13. The symbol $^{238}_{92}U$ shows that this uranium atom contains

    A. 238 protons and 92 electrons

    B. 92 protons and 146 neutrons

    C. 92 protons and 238 neutrons

    D. 146 protons and 92 neutrons.

14. An atom contains 8 protons, 10 neutrons and 8 electrons.

Which of the following represents the atom?

A. $_{8}^{16}X$ B. $_{8}^{18}X$ C. $_{10}^{18}X$ D. $_{10}^{26}X$

Question 15 and 16 refer to the information in the table below.

Element	W	X	Y	Z
Atomic number	9	19	18	20
Mass number	19	39	40	40

15. Which elements have the same number of electrons?

A. W and X   B. X and Z

C. Y and Z   D. none of these

16. Which elements have the same number of neutrons?

A. W and X   B. X and Z

C. Y and Z   D. none of these

Credit level

1. Isotopes of the same element must have

    A.   the same number of protons and neutrons, but different numbers of electrons

    B.   the same number of protons and electrons, but different numbers of neutrons

    C.   the same number of neutrons, but different numbers of protons and electrons

    D.   the same number of protons, but different numbers of electrons and neutrons.

2. Some atoms of an element are heavier than other atoms of the same element.

    This is because they have different numbers of

    A.   neutrons   B.   protons   C.   nuclei   D.   electrons.

3. Which of the following statements is **not** true about isotopes?

    A.   Their electron arrangements are the same.

    B.   The masses of their nuclei are different.

    C.   Their numbers of protons are different.

    D.   Their nuclear charges are the same.

4. The two isotopes of carbon, $^{12}_{6}C$ and $^{14}_{6}C$, differ from each other in

    A.   mass number   B.   atomic number

    C.   chemical properties   D.   electron arrangement.

5. An isotope of oxygen of mass number 18 differs from the most abundant form of oxygen in

    A.   the number of atoms per molecule

    B.   the number of electrons in the outer energy level (shell)

    C.   the number of protons in each nucleus

    D.   the ratio of neutrons to protons in the nucleus.

In questions 6 to 11, decide whether each of the following pairs of atoms are

    A. isotopes of the same element   **B.** **NOT** isotopes of the same element.

6.   an atom with 6 protons and 8 neutrons
and
an atom with 8 protons and 8 neutrons

7.   an atom with 10 protons and 10 neutrons
and
an atom with 10 protons and 12 neutrons.

8.   an atom with atomic number 17 and mass number 35
and
an atom with atomic number 17 and mass number 37

9.   an atom with atomic number 1 and mass number 2
and
an atom with atomic number 2 and mass number 4

10. $^{16}_{8}\text{W}$ and $^{18}_{8}\text{X}$

11. $^{40}_{19}\text{Y}$ and $^{40}_{20}\text{Z}$

12.   Which pair or pairs of the following atoms are isotopes of the same element?

     $^{86}_{38}\text{W}$ $^{86}_{36}\text{X}$ $^{87}_{38}\text{Y}$ $^{87}_{37}\text{Z}$

     A. **W, X** only   **B.** **W, Y** only   **C.** **W, X** and **Y, Z**   **D.** no pair

13.

Atom	Number of neutrons in nucleus	Nuclear charge
1	50	36
2	50	37
3	49	38
4	52	38

From the information given in the table above, which of the following pairs of atoms are isotopes?

     A. 1 and 2   **B.** 2 and 3   **C.** 2 and 4   **D.** 3 and 4

14.   An isotope of an element can be represented $^{50}_{24}\text{X}$.

Which of the following is most likely to represent another isotope of the element?

     A. $^{50}_{23}\text{X}$ **B.** $^{52}_{24}\text{X}$ **C.** $^{82}_{24}\text{X}$ **D.** $^{50}_{25}\text{X}$

Test 3.9   Relative atomic mass (atomic weight)

Credit level

The relative atomic mass of an element is rarely a whole number.

In questions 1 to 5, decide whether each of the following statements is

    A. an explanation of this fact

    B. NOT an explanation of this fact.

1.   Different atoms of an element can have different numbers of protons.

2.   It is difficult to isolate pure elements.

3.   Most elements consist of a mixture of isotopes.

4.   Chemical methods of determining the relative atomic masses of elements are inaccurate.

5.   Different atoms of an element can have different numbers of neutrons.

6.   An element consists of two isotopes with mass numbers 40 and 42.

     The relative atomic mass **must** be

    A. 41 exactly

    B. more than 41

    C. less than 41

    D. between 40 and 42, but impossible to specify.

7.   The relative atomic mass of lithium is 6.94.

     This is because

    A.   all lithium atoms have a mass of 6.94 amu

    B.   most lithium atoms have a mass of 7 amu but a few have a mass of 6 amu

    C.   most lithium atoms have a mass of 6 amu but a few have a mass of 7 amu.

8.   Copper has two isotopes, each with a percentage abundance as shown:

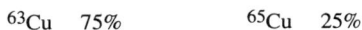

         ^{63}Cu 75% ^{65}Cu 25%

     What is the approximate relative atomic mass of copper?

    A.   63   **B.**   63.5   **C.**   64   **D.**   65

General level

In questions 1 to 12, decide whether each of the following compounds is

    A. made up of molecules

    B. **NOT** made up of molecules.

1.	sodium chloride	7.	aluminum oxide
2.	hydrogen oxide	8.	calcium iodide
3.	magnesium sulphide	9.	nitrogen fluoride
4.	carbon tetrachloride	10.	lithium hydroxide
5.	hydrogen fluoride	11.	zinc nitrate
6.	potassium carbonate	12.	sulphur trioxide

In questions 13 to 24, decide whether each of the following elements

    A. exists as diatomic molecules

    B. does **NOT** exist as diatomic molecules.

13.	hydrogen	19.	fluorine
14.	magnesium	20.	nitrogen
15.	carbon	21.	neon
16.	oxygen	22.	bromine
17.	chlorine	23.	iron
18.	sulphur	24.	iodine

Credit level

Decide the shape of each of the following molecules.

1. nitrogen hydride

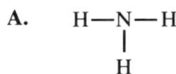

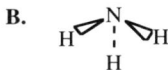

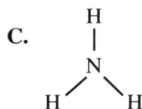

    A.   H—N—H
             |
             H

    B.   (structure showing N with H atoms)

    C.   (pyramidal structure with N and three H)

2. hydrogen oxide

    A.   (bent structure O with two H)

    B.   H—O—H

    C.   H—O
               |
               H

3. carbon fluoride

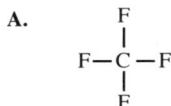

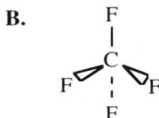

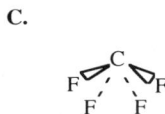

    A.   F
             |
        F—C—F
             |
             F

    B.   (structure with C and four F)

    C.   (structure with C and four F)

4. carbon dioxide

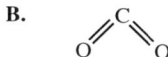

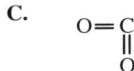

    A.   O=C=O

    B.   (bent structure C with two O)

    C.   O=C
               ‖
               O

5. hydrogen sulphide

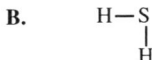

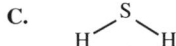

    A.   H—S—H

    B.   H—S
               |
               H

    C.   (bent structure S with two H)

6. silicon chloride

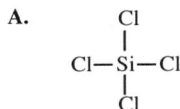

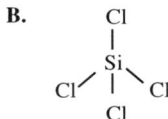

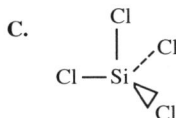

    A.   Cl
             |
        Cl—Si—Cl
             |
             Cl

    B.   Cl
             |
             Si
         Cl / | \ Cl
             Cl

    C.   Cl
             | Cl
        Cl—Si
             Cl

7. phosphorus hydride

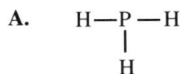

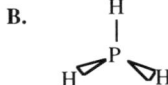

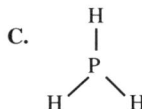

    A.   H—P—H
             |
             H

    B.   H
             |
             P
         H /   \ H

    C.   H
             |
             P
         H /   \ H

General level

1. What gas is the main component of the air?

   A. hydrogen   **B.** nitrogen

   C. oxygen   **D.** carbon dioxide

2. What is the approximate percentage of oxygen in the air?

   A. 20%   **B.** 40%   **C.** 60%   **D.** 80%

3. Which of the following tests can be used to distinguish oxygen from other gases?

   A. It burns with a 'pop'.   **B.** It relights a glowing splint.

   C. It turns lime water milky.   **D.** It puts out a burning splint.

Questions 4 and 5 refer to the result of testing four different gases with a burning splint.

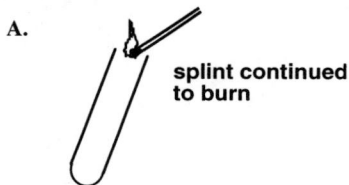

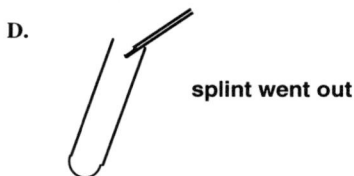

A. splint continued to burn

B. gas in test tube burned

C. splint burned more brightly

D. splint went out

4. Which gas is oxygen?

5. Which gas could be butane?

6. What fuel makes up 95% of natural gas?

   A. methane   **B.** ethane   **C.** propane   **D.** butane

In questions 7 to 12, decide whether each of the following sources of energy is

    A. a finite resource   **B.** a renewable source.

7.   solar power   10.   oil

8.   coal   11.   natural gas

9.   hydro-electricity   12.   tidal power

In questions 13 to 22, decide whether each of the following substances

    A. can be used as a fuel   **B.** can **NOT** be used as a fuel.

13.   wood   18.   water

14.   glass   19.   coke

15.   peat   20.   nitrogen

16.   petrol   21.   hydrogen

17.   sand   22.   carbon dioxide

In questions 23 to 30, decide whether each of the following sources of energy

    A. can be classified as a fossil fuel

    B. can **NOT** be classified as a fossil fuel.

23.   coal   27.   solar

24.   oil   28.   peat

25.   electricity   29.   wood

26.   natural gas   30.   nuclear

General level

1. The fractional distillation of crude petroleum oil depends on the fact that the different fractions have different

   A. ignition temperatures   **B.** boiling points

   C. solubilities   **D.** densities.

2. Which two changes of state occur when petrol is obtained from crude oil?

   A. melting followed by evaporation   **B.** condensation followed by evaporation

   C. evaporation followed by condensation **D.** condensation followed by freezing

Question 3 to 6 are about uses of the products of fractional distillation of crude oil.

     A. diesel   **B.** bitumen   **C.** kerosene   **D.** lubricating oil

3. Which product is used to tar roads?

4. Which product is used as a fuel for jet aeroplanes?

5. Which product is used to reduce friction and wear in car engines?

6. Which product is used to as a fuel for trains and certain cars?

Questions 7 to 13 refer to properties of fractions, collected over the temperature ranges shown.

Fraction	Temperature range / °C
1	less than 40
2	40 - 75
3	150 - 240
4	220 - 250
5	250 - 350
6	>350

Decide whether each of the following statements about the properties of the fractions is

     A. TRUE   **B.** FALSE.

7. Fraction 3 is more viscous than fraction 6.

8. Fraction 2 is more volatile than fraction 4.

9. Fraction 3 is less flammable than fraction 6.

10. Fraction 5 is thicker than fraction 3.

11. Fraction 1 has a higher boiling point than fraction 4.

12. Fraction 2 burns more easily than fraction 5.

13. Fraction 3 boils at a lower temperature than fraction 5.

In questions 14 to 20, decide whether each of the following statements about the properties of distillation fractions is

A. TRUE   **B.** FALSE.

14.   Petrol is more viscous than diesel.

15.   Lubricating oil is more volatile than bitumen.

16.   Diesel is less flammable than the gas fraction.

17.   Bitumen is thicker than kerosine.

18.   The gas fraction has a higher boiling point than lubricating oil.

19.   Petrol burns more easily than diesel.

20.   Kerosine boils at a lower temperature than bitumen.

Credit level

Questions 21 to 26 refer to the following ranges of chain length.

A. C_1 to C_4 **B.** C_4 to C_{12}

C. C_9 to C_{16} **D.** C_{15} to C_{25}

E. C_{20} to C_{70} **F.** greater than C_{70}

Decide which range is typical of the molecules found in each of the following fractions.

21.   petrol

22.   bitumen

23.   kerosine

24.   the gas fraction

25.   lubricating oil

26.   diesel

Test 5.3

Burning of hydrocarbons (i)

General level

1. What test is used to distinguish carbon dioxide from other gases?

   A.   It puts out a burning splint.

   B.   It is soluble in water.

   C.   It turns damp pH paper red.

   D.   It turns lime water milky.

2. In which of the following ways can water be distinguished from other liquids?

   A.   It is colourless and does not smell.

   B.   It does not change the colour of universal indicator.

   C.   It has a melting point of 0 °C and a boiling point of 100 °C.

   D.   It is not flammable.

3. When a hydrocarbon burns in a plentiful supply of air, the products are

   A.   carbon and hydrogen

   B.   carbon and water vapour

   C.   carbon dioxide and hydrogen

   D.   carbon dioxide and water vapour.

4. The presence of carbon monoxide in car exhaust gases is mainly because

   A.   the combustion of the hydrocarbons in the petrol in the engine is incomplete

   B.   the hydrocarbons in petrol form carbon monoxide on complete combustion

   C.   the carbon dioxide produced by complete combustion is changed to carbon monoxide by heat

   D.   some of the hydrocarbons in petrol decompose to form carbon monoxide.

5. It is inadvisable to burn paraffin in a poorly ventilated room because

   A.   poisonous hydrocarbons are formed

   B.   a mixture of paraffin and air is explosive

   C.   the incomplete combustion of paraffin results in the formation of hydrogen

   D.   a shortage of oxygen may result in the formation of carbon monoxide.

6. Which compound can be present in car exhaust fumes because of a reaction between the gases in the air?

    A. carbon monoxide   **B.** carbon dioxide

    C. sulphur dioxide   **D.** nitrogen dioxide

7. Compounds of which element are present in some exhaust fumes because of substances which are added to help the petrol burn?

    A. carbon   **B.** nitrogen   **C.** sulphur   **D.** lead

Questions 8 to 11 refer to the formula for substances found in exhaust fumes.

Decide whether the presence of each of the following substances is

    A. a result of incomplete combustion of petrol

    B. **NOT** a result of incomplete combustion of petrol.

8. C

9. CO_2

10. CO

11. C_8H_{18}

In questions 12 to 16, decide whether each of the following gases is

    A. poisonous   **B.** non poisonous.

12. carbon monoxide

13. water vapour

14. nitrogen dioxide

15. sulphur dioxide

16. carbon dioxide

17. Which element can be obtained from compounds found in oil or natural gas?

    A. chlorine   **B.** phosphorus

    C. silicon   **D.** sulphur

Credit level

Question 1 and 2 refer to different molecules.

1. When a sample of gas is burned carbon dioxide is formed.

   What **must** this gas be made up of?

   A. molecules containing carbon atoms

   B. molecules of hydrocarbons

   C. molecules of carbon monoxide

   D. molecules containing hydrogen atoms

2. When a sample of gas is burned water is formed.

   What **must** this gas be made up of?

   A. molecules of hydrocarbons

   B. molecules containing carbon atoms

   C. molecules of carbon monoxide

   D. molecules containing hydrogen atoms

3. The products of burning lighter fuel in air are water and carbon dioxide.

   This shows that molecules of lighter fuel contain

   A. carbon atoms and water molecules

   B. hydrogen atoms and carbon dioxide molecules

   C. hydrogen atoms and carbon atoms

   D. water molecules and carbon dioxide molecules.

4. When a cold dry surface was held over a burning fuel, drops of water condensed on it.

   The fuel could contain

   A. carbon monoxide

   B. a hydrocarbon

   C. carbon dioxide

   D. carbon.

5. When a drop of lime water was held over a burning fuel, the lime water turned milky.

   Which of the following would **not** burn to produce this result?

   A. hydrogen

   B. carbon monoxide

   C. a hydrocarbon

   D. carbon

6. Which of the following families of elements is used in exhaust systems to reduce air pollution?

    A. the noble gases   **B.** the alkali metals

    C. the halogens   **D.** the transition metals

7. In car engines, the efficiency of combustion of hydrocarbons is improved by

    A. increasing the fuel to air ratio

    B. removing nitrogen fron the air before combustion

    C. adding a catalyst to the petrol in the engine

    D. decreasing the fuel to air ratio.

Question 8 to 10 refer to the table below.

This shows the approximate compositions of five gaseous fuels.

	% hydrogen	% nitrogen	% hydrocarbon	% carbon monoxide
Fuel A	50	-	-	50
Fuel B	-	-	95-100	-
Fuel C	-	67	-	33
Fuel D	50	3	37	10
Fuel E	100	-	-	-

8. Which fuel will burn to give **only** water?

9. Which **two** fuels will **not** burn to give carbon dioxide and water?

10. Which fuel would be expected to produce least heat energy when equal volumes of the fuel are burned?

General level

In questions 1 to 12, decide whether each of the following hydrocarbons is

    A. an alkane   **B.** an alkene

    C. saturated   **D.** unsaturated.

(Note that for each question, TWO responses should be given.)

1. ethane

2. propene

3. pentene

4. octane

5.

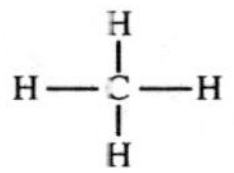

6.

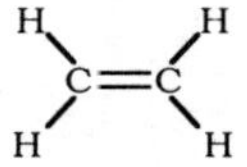

7.

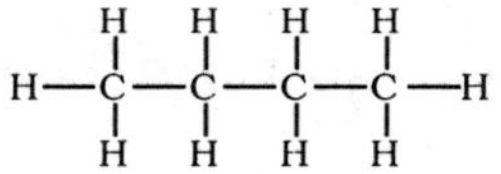

8.

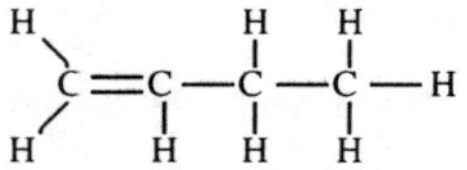

9. C_3H_8

10. C_5H_{10} (straight-chain)

11. $C_{16}H_{32}$ (straight-chain)

12. $C_{20}H_{42}$

Question 13 to 16 refer to the following structures.

A.

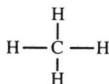

B.

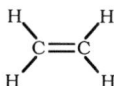

C

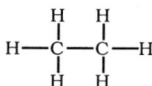

D.

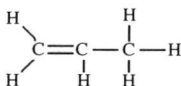

E.

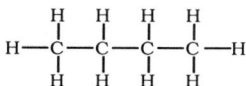

F.

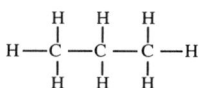

G.

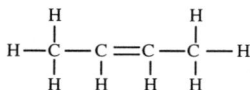

13.   What is the structure of ethane?

14.   What is the structure of butene?

15.   What is the structure of methane?

16.   What is the structure of propene?

Questions 17 to 20 refer to hydrocarbons with the following formulae.

    A. C_5H_{12} **B.** C_6H_{14} **C.** C_7H_{16} **D.** C_8H_{18}

17.   What is the formula for octane?

18.   What is the formula for pentane?

19.   What is the formula for heptane?

20.   What is the formula for hexane?

21.   How many hydrogen atoms are in a straight-chain alkane with 25 carbon atoms?

    A.   48   **B.**   50   **C.**   52   **D.**   54

22.   How many hydrogen atoms are in a straight-chain alkene with 12 carbon atoms?

    A.   20   **B.**   22   **C.**   24   **D.**   26

General level

In questions 1 to 12, decide whether each of the following hydrocarbons

    A. reacts quickly with bromine

    B. does **NOT** react quickly with bromine.

1. butene

2. hexane

3. butane

4. pentene

5.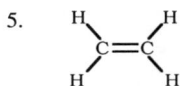

6.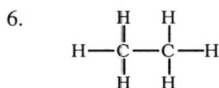

7.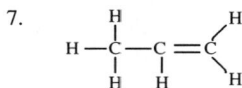

8.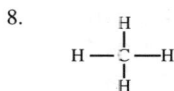

9. C_3H_8

10. C_6H_{12} (straight-chain)

11. C_8H_{18}

12. $C_{10}H_{20}$ (straight-chain)

Questions 13 to 15 refer to the reaction of alkenes wih bromine.

(Note that for questions 13 and 14, more than one response is correct.)

13. Which of the following represents the product of the reaction between ethene and bromine?

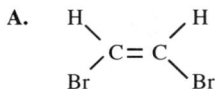

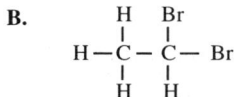

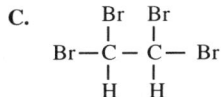

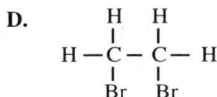

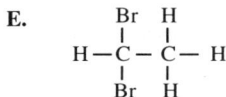

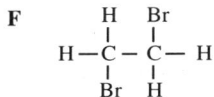

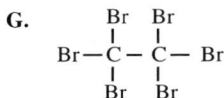

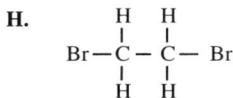

A.
$$\text{C}=\text{C} \text{ with H, H on left carbon; Br, Br substituents}$$

H   H
 \\ /
  C = C
 / \\
Br   Br

B.
```
    H   Br
    |   |
H — C — C — Br
    |   |
    H   H
```

C.
```
   Br  Br
    |   |
Br—C — C — Br
    |   |
    H   H
```

D.
```
    H   H
    |   |
H — C — C — H
    |   |
    Br  Br
```

E.
```
    Br  H
    |   |
H — C — C — H
    |   |
    Br  H
```

F
```
    H   Br
    |   |
H — C — C — H
    |   |
    Br  H
```

G.
```
   Br  Br
    |   |
Br—C — C — Br
    |   |
   Br  Br
```

H.
```
    H   H
    |   |
Br—C — C — Br
    |   |
    H   H
```

14. Which of the following represents the product of the reaction between propene and bromine?

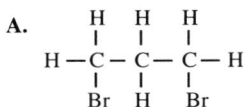

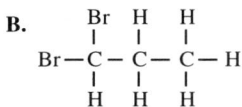

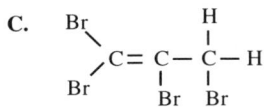

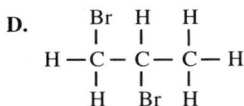

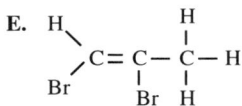

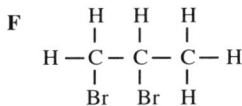

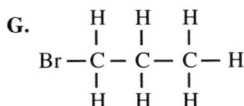

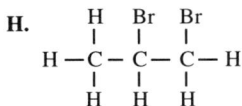

A.
```
    H   H   H
    |   |   |
H — C — C — C — H
    |   |   |
    Br  H   Br
```

B.
```
    Br  H   H
    |   |   |
Br—C — C — C — H
    |   |   |
    H   H   H
```

C.
```
   Br              H
    \\              |
     C = C — C — H
    /          |   |
   Br          Br  Br
```

D.
```
    Br  H   H
    |   |   |
H — C — C — C — H
    |   |   |
    H   Br  H
```

E.
```
   H              H
    \\             |
     C = C — C — H
    /          |   |
   Br          Br  H
```

F
```
    H   H   H
    |   |   |
H — C — C — C — H
    |   |   |
    Br  Br  H
```

G.
```
    H   H   H
    |   |   |
Br—C — C — C — H
    |   |   |
    H   H   H
```

H.
```
    H   Br  Br
    |   |   |
H — C — C — C — H
    |   |   |
    H   H   H
```

Structure and reactions of hydrocarbons   37

15. What kind of reaction takes place when butene decolourises bromine?

   A. distillation   **B.** addition

   C. evaporation   **D.** condensation

Questions 16 to 18 refer to the reaction of alkenes with hydrogen.

16. What is formed when ethene reacts with hydrogen?

   A. methane   **B.** ethane   **C.** propene   **D.** propane

17. What is formed when butene reacts with hydrogen?

   A. propene   **B.** propane   **C.** butane   **D.** pentene

18. Which hydrocarbon reacts with hydrogen to form hexane?

   A. propene   **B.** pentane   **C.** hexene   **D.** octane.

General level

Questions l to 20 refer to the experiment shown in the diagram opposite.

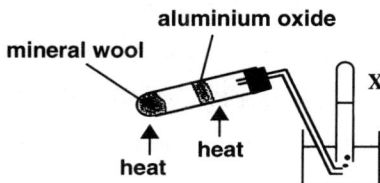

In the apparatus, the mineral wool was soaked with a liquid alkane, $C_{12}H_{26}$. Its vapour was passed over hot aluminium oxide and gas **X** was collected by displacement of water.

Decide whether each of the following statements is

      A. TRUE   **B.** FALSE.

1. The reaction taking place is called distillation.

2. The aluminium oxide is changed to aluminium.

3. The gas collected is insoluble in water.

4. The aluminium oxide acts as a catalyst.

5. The gas collected burns to give both water and carbon dioxide.

6. Only methane gas is produced.

7. The aluminium oxide gradually melts.

8. The reaction taking place is called addition.

9. The gas collected quickly decolourises bromine.

10. There is no change in the chemical composition of the aluminium oxide.

11. The gas collected **could** contain ethene.

12. The gas collected turns lime water milky.

13. The gas collected burns to give only water.

14. The aluminium oxide is changed to aluminium carbonate.

15. The reaction taking place is called cracking.

16. The gas collected contains a mixture of hydrocarbons.

17. The gas collected burns to give only carbon dioxide.

18. The gas collected contains unsaturated molecules.

19. Molecules with the formula $C_{13}H_{26}$ are found in the gas.

20. The gas collected **could** contain ethane.

Structure and reactions of hydrocarbons

21. A liquid hydrocarbon had no visible effect on bromine, but when it was cracked the gas produced decolourised bromine.

This is because

A. gases decolourise bromine; liquids do not

B. the gas formed was unsaturated; the liquid was not

C. the gas formed was at a higher temperature than the liquid

D. the gas formed by the cracking was not a hydrocarbon.

22. The hydrocarbon $C_{16}H_{34}$ is cracked as shown in the equation below.

$$C_{16}H_{34} \quad \rightarrow \quad C_{10}H_{20} \quad + \quad X$$

What is the formula for X?

A. C_6H_{14} B. $C_{10}H_{22}$ C. $C_{16}H_{32}$ D. $C_{26}H_{54}$

23. The hydrocarbon $C_{10}H_{22}$ is cracked as shown in the equation below.

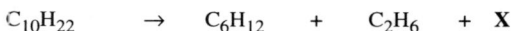

$$C_{10}H_{22} \quad \rightarrow \quad C_6H_{12} \quad + \quad C_2H_6 \quad + \quad X$$

X must be

A. methane   B. ethene

C. propane   D. butene.

24. Hexane can be cracked to give ethene and another hydrocarbon.

The other hydrocarbon must be

A. propane   B. propene

C. butane   D. butene.

25. A C_{11} alkane is cracked into pentane and two other straight-chain hydrocarbons.

If one of these is ethene, the other must be

A. propane   B. propene

C. butane   D. butene.

Test 6.4

Structure and reactions of hydrocarbons

Credit level

Questions 1 and 2 refer to the following structures.

A.

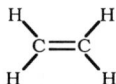

B.

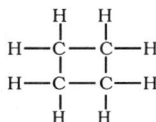

C.

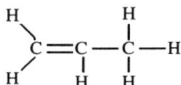

D.

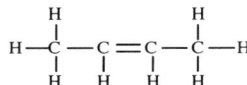

1.   Which is **not** an alkene?

2.   Which is a saturated hydrocarbon?

Questions 3 to 8 refer to the following formulae for hydrocarbons.

    A. C_5H_{10} **B.** C_5H_{12} **C.** C_6H_{12} **D.** C_6H_{14}

What is the formula for each of the following hydrocarbons?

3.   hexane

4.   pentene

5.   cyclohexane

6.   pentane

7.   hexene

8.   cyclopentane

9.   How many hydrogen atoms are in the cycloalkane with 20 carbon atoms?

    A.   38   **B.**   40   **C.**   42   **D.**   44

10.   Which one of the following could **not** be either a straight-chain alkane or a cycloalkane?

    A. C_4H_{10} **B.** C_5H_{10} **C.** C_6H_{12} **D.** C_6H_{10}

Structure and reactions of hydrocarbons

41

In questions 11 to 13, decide which hydrocarbon is **not** a member of the same homologous series as the others.

11. **A.** ethene   **B.** hexene   **C.** butene   **D.** cyclopropane

12. **A.** butane   **B.** methane   **C.** octane   **D.** cyclohexane

13. **A.** C_3H_8 **B.** C_5H_{12} **C.** C_6H_{12} **D.** C_7H_{16}

14. Which hydrocarbon is a member of the same homologous series as the compound represented by the formula C_4H_{10}?

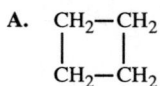

    A.
$$\begin{array}{c} CH_2-CH_2 \\ |\qquad| \\ CH_2-CH_2 \end{array}$$

    B. $CH_3-CH=CH_2$

    C. $CH_2=CH_2$

    D. CH_4

15. Which compound has the general formula $C_nH_{2n}O$?

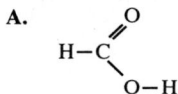

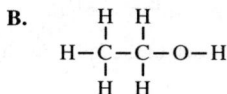

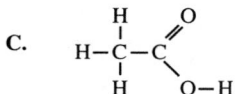

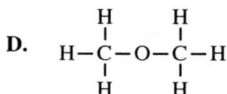

16. Which compound belongs to a series with the general formula $C_nH_{2n}S$?

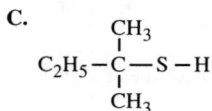

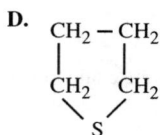

    A. CH_3-S-CH_3 **B.** $CH_3-S-C_2H_5$

    C.
$$\begin{array}{c} CH_3 \\ | \\ C_2H_5-C-S-H \\ | \\ CH_3 \end{array}$$

    D.
$$\begin{array}{c} CH_2-CH_2 \\ |\qquad\quad| \\ CH_2\quad CH_2 \\ \diagdown\;\diagup \\ S \end{array}$$

17. Which of the following hydrocarbons reacts quickly with bromine?

   A. butane

   B. cyclobutane

   C. butene

   D. none of these

18. Which of the following hydrocarbons does **not** react quickly with bromine?

   A.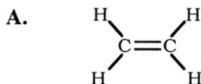

   B.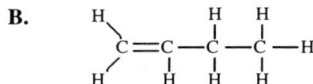

   C.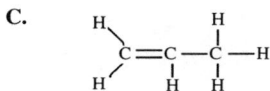

   D.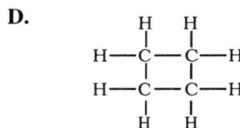

19. A hydrocarbon, molecular formula C_5H_{10} does **not** quickly decolourise bromine.

   Which of the following could it be?

   A. pentane

   B. pentene

   C. cyclopentane

   D. none of these

20. When a molecule of the hydrocarbon $CH_2=CH-CH=CH_2$ completely reacts with bromine, the number of molecules of bromine used would be

   A. 1   B. 2   C. 4   D. 8.

Credit level

(Note that for some questions in this test, there may not be any compounds which can be picked out. In this case, the answer NONE should be given.)

Questions 1 to 3 refer to the structures shown below.

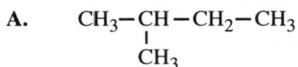

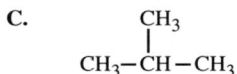

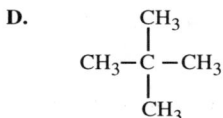

A. $CH_3-CH-CH_2-CH_3$
            $|$
            CH_3

B. $CH_3-CH_2-CH_2-CH_2-CH_2-CH_3$

C. CH_3
               $|$
      $CH_3-CH-CH_3$

D. CH_3
               $|$
      CH_3-C-CH_3
               $|$
              CH_3

Pick out **all** the hydrocarbons that are isomers of each of the following structures.

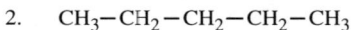

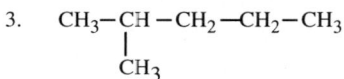

1. $CH_3-CH_2-CH_2-CH_3$

2. $CH_3-CH_2-CH_2-CH_2-CH_3$

3. $CH_3-CH-CH_2-CH_2-CH_3$
            $|$
            CH_3

Questions 4 and 5 refer to the structures shown below.

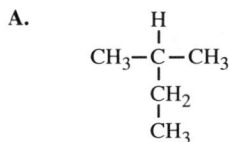

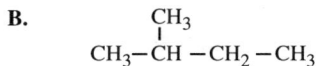

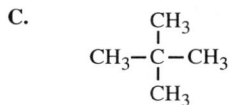

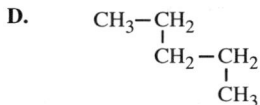

A.
$$
\begin{array}{c}
\text{H} \\
| \\
\text{CH}_3-\text{C}-\text{CH}_3 \\
| \\
\text{CH}_2 \\
| \\
\text{CH}_3
\end{array}
$$

B.
$$
\begin{array}{c}
\text{CH}_3 \\
| \\
\text{CH}_3-\text{CH}-\text{CH}_2-\text{CH}_3
\end{array}
$$

C.
$$
\begin{array}{c}
\text{CH}_3 \\
| \\
\text{CH}_3-\text{C}-\text{CH}_3 \\
| \\
\text{CH}_3
\end{array}
$$

D.
$$
\begin{array}{c}
\text{CH}_3-\text{CH}_2 \\
| \\
\text{CH}_2-\text{CH}_2 \\
| \\
\text{CH}_3
\end{array}
$$

Pick out **all** the hydrocarbons that are isomers of each of the following structures.

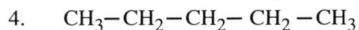

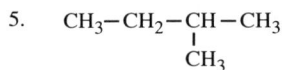

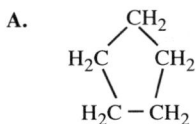

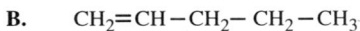

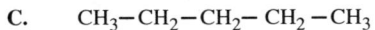

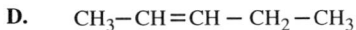

4. $CH_3-CH_2-CH_2-CH_2-CH_3$

5. $CH_3-CH_2-CH-CH_3$
    $\quad\quad\quad\quad\quad | $
    $\quad\quad\quad\quad\;\; CH_3$

6. Pick out **all** the hydrocarbons that are isomers of the following structure:

    $CH_3-CH_2-CH_2-CH=CH_2$

A.
$$
\begin{array}{c}
\quad\;\text{CH}_2 \\
\diagup \quad \diagdown \\
\text{H}_2\text{C} \quad\quad \text{CH}_2 \\
\diagdown \quad\; \diagup \\
\text{H}_2\text{C}-\text{CH}_2
\end{array}
$$

B. $CH_2=CH-CH_2-CH_2-CH_3$

C. $CH_3-CH_2-CH_2-CH_2-CH_3$

D. $CH_3-CH=CH-CH_2-CH_3$

Questions 7 and 8 refer to the structures shown below.

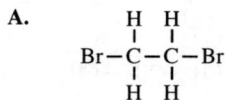

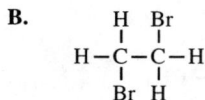

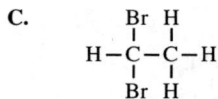

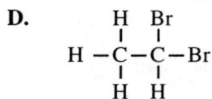

A.
$$Br-\underset{\underset{H}{|}}{\overset{\overset{H}{|}}{C}}-\underset{\underset{H}{|}}{\overset{\overset{H}{|}}{C}}-Br$$

B.
$$H-\underset{\underset{Br}{|}}{\overset{\overset{H}{|}}{C}}-\underset{\underset{H}{|}}{\overset{\overset{Br}{|}}{C}}-H$$

C.
$$H-\underset{\underset{Br}{|}}{\overset{\overset{Br}{|}}{C}}-\underset{\underset{H}{|}}{\overset{\overset{H}{|}}{C}}-H$$

D.
$$H-\underset{\underset{H}{|}}{\overset{\overset{H}{|}}{C}}-\underset{\underset{H}{|}}{\overset{\overset{Br}{|}}{C}}-Br$$

Pick out **all** the compounds that are isomers of each of the following structures.

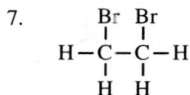

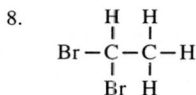

7.
$$H-\underset{\underset{H}{|}}{\overset{\overset{Br}{|}}{C}}-\underset{\underset{H}{|}}{\overset{\overset{Br}{|}}{C}}-H$$

8.
$$Br-\underset{\underset{Br}{|}}{\overset{\overset{H}{|}}{C}}-\underset{\underset{H}{|}}{\overset{\overset{H}{|}}{C}}-H$$

Questions 9 and 10 refer to the structures shown below.

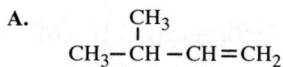

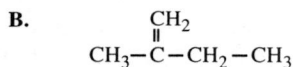

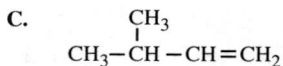

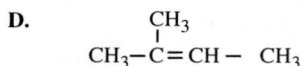

A.
$$CH_3-\underset{\underset{CH_3}{|}}{CH}-CH=CH_2$$

B.
$$CH_3-\underset{\overset{||}{CH_2}}{C}-CH_2-CH_3$$

C.
$$CH_3-\underset{\underset{CH_3}{|}}{CH}-CH=CH_2$$

D.
$$CH_3-\underset{\underset{CH_3}{|}}{C}=CH-\ CH_3$$

Pick out **all** the hydrocarbons that are isomers of each of the following structures.

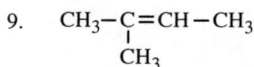

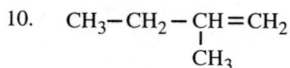

9.
$$CH_3-\underset{\underset{CH_3}{|}}{C}=CH-CH_3$$

10.
$$CH_3-CH_2-\underset{\underset{CH_3}{|}}{CH}=CH_2$$

General level

Questions 1 to 10 refer to the ability of **elements** to conduct electricity.

Decide whether each of the following

A. conducts electricity   **B.** does **NOT** conduct electricity.

1.	zinc solid	6.	iodine solid
2.	sulphur solid	7.	liquid mercury
3.	carbon (graphite) solid	8.	titanium solid
4.	molten iron	9.	argon solid
5.	liquid oxygen	10.	molten lead

Questions 11 to 25 refer to the ability of **compounds** to conduct electricity.

Decide whether each of the following

A. conducts electricity   **B.** does **NOT** conduct electricity.

11.	calcium chloride solid	19.	silicon oxide solid
12.	phosphorus pentachloride solid	20.	carbon dioxide solid
13.	sodium bromide solution	21.	magnesium sulphide solid
14.	copper oxide solid	22.	sodium bromide melt
15.	lead iodide melt	23.	liquid hexene (C_6H_{12})
16.	iron chloride solution	24.	solid paraffin wax $(C_{24}H_{50})$
17.	liquid ethanol (C_2H_5OH)	25.	a solution of methanol (CH_3OH)
18.	a solution of sucrose $(C_{12}H_{22}O_{11})$		

Question 26 to 31 refer to the table below which shows the ability of substances to conduct electricity.

	Solid	Liquid/melt
A.	No	No
B.	No	Yes
C.	Yes	Yes

Which of the above could be applied to each of the following substances?

26. calcium chloride

27. mercury

28. phenol (C_6H_6O)

29. lead

30. sodium bromide

31. octane (C_8H_{18})

Questions 32 and 33 refer to the following substances.

    A. iron   **B.** sulphur

    C. lead chloride   **D.** silicon chloride

32. Which substance does **not** conduct electricity as a solid but does conduct electricity when molten?

33. Which substance conducts electricity both as a solid and melt?

General level

Questions 1 to 12 refer to types of bonding found in compounds.

      A. ionic   **B.** covalent

Which type of bonding is found in each of the following compounds?

1.   sulphur fluoride

2.   sodium iodide

3.   magnesium chloride

4.   carbon tetrachloride

5.   CaO

6. V_2O_5

7. SiH_4

8. C_3H_6O

9.   a compound which is made up of molecules

10.   a compound which is a liquid at room temperature

11.   a compound which is made up of a network of oppositely charged particles

12.   a compound with a boiling point of 25 $^\circ$C?

13.   Which type of bonding is more likely to be found in a compound which is soluble in water?

      A. ionic   **B.** covalent

General / Credit level

1. Consider the following table which shows the colour of solutions.

Metal ion	Sulphate	Chloride	Nitrate	Dichromate
X	blue	blue	blue	green
Y	colourless	colourless	colourless	yellow

Which of the following statements is true?

A. The nitrate ion is blue.

B. Ions of **Y** are yellow.

C. The dichromate ion is green.

D. Ions of **X** are blue.

Question 2 to 6 refer to the data shown below.

Compound	Melting point	Type of bonding
A.	over 500 $^{\circ}$C	ionic
B.	over 500 $^{\circ}$C	covalent
C.	under 0 $^{\circ}$C	covalent

Which set of data is most likely to be true of each of the following compounds?

2. radium chloride

3. selenium chloride

4. nickel bromide

5. silicon dioxide

6. hydrogen sulphide

Questions 7 to 9 refer to the information in the following table.

Substance	Melting point / $^{\circ}$C	Boiling point / $^{\circ}$C	Conduct as	
			a solid	a liquid
A.	963	1560	no	yes
B.	1455	2730	yes	yes
C.	-183	-164	no	no
D.	1700	2230	no	no

7. Which substance is ionic?

8. Which substance is a covalent network substance?

9. Which substance is made up of molecules?

General / Credit level

Questions 1 to 7 refer to the electrolysis of copper chloride solution.

In questions 1 to 3, decide whether each of the following states of copper chloride is

    A. suitable for electrolysis

    B. NOT suitable for electrolysis.

1.   solid

2.   solution

3.   melt

In questions 4 to 7, decide whether each of the following statements is

    A. TRUE   **B.** FALSE.

4.   Copper ions lose electrons at the negative electrode.

5.   Copper ions gain electrons at the positive electrode.

6.   Chloride ions lose electrons at the positive electrode.

7.   Chloride ions gain electrons at the negative electrode.

In questions 8 to 11, decide whether each of the following solutions

    A. can be used as an electrolyte

    B. can **NOT** be used as an electrolyte.

8.   NaBr

9. C_2H_5OH

10. $C_{12}H_{22}O_{11}$

11. $NiCl_2$

Questions 12 and 13 refer to the following substances.

    A. iodine   **B.** glucose $(C_6H_{12}O_6)$

    C. lead   **D.** sodium bromide

To which substance does each of the following statements apply?

12.   When an electric current is passed through the molten substance no decomposition occurs.

13.   The passage of an electric current through the molten substance results in decomposition.

Questions 14 and 15 refer to the following experiment.

A crystal is placed on a piece of moist filter paper and a current of electricity passed as shown in the diagram.

The following compounds were used in the experiment.

A. calcium chloride **B.** potassium sulphate

C. sodium permanganate **D.** copper nitrate

14. Which crystal would result in a colour moving towards the positive electrode?

15. Which crystal would result in a colour moving towards the negative electrode?

16. Solid potassium iodide does not conduct electricity because

A. its ions are not free to move

B. it is a covalent compound

C. it does not contain enough ions to carry the current

D. it contains no electrons.

17. A pupil wrote the following statement:

"When an electric current is passed through a solution of ethanol (C_2H_5OH), no decomposition occurs"

This statement is wrong because

A. decomposition of the ethanol does occur

B. no appreciable current can flow in the solution

C. is should be stated that the ethanol breaks up to form ions

D. ethanol does not dissolve in water.

18. Although solid sodium chloride does not conduct electricity, a solution of the sodium chloride in water carries current because

A. ions are produced when the current is switched on

B. ions are produced when the sodium chloride is dissolved in water

C. water is a good conductor of electricity

D. ions are freed when the sodium chloride is dissolved in water.

Questions 19 to 23 refer to the electrolysis of copper(II) dichromate solution.

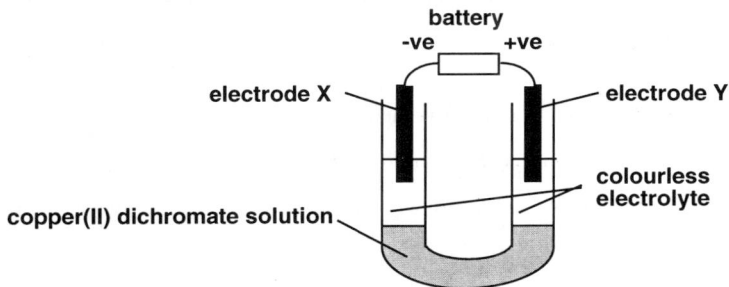

Copper(II) dichromate solution contains blue copper ions and orange dichromate ions.

Decide whether each of the following statements is

    A. TRUE   **B.** FALSE.

19. Copper forms at electrode **X**.

20. The electrolyte around electrode **X** remains colourless.

21. A blue colour moves to electrode **Y**.

22. Dichromate ions move to electrode **Y**.

23. Electrons move through the solution from **X** to **Y**.

24. Which of the following diagrams shows best the relationship between conductors, electrolytes, metals, non-conductors and non-electrolytes.

  A.

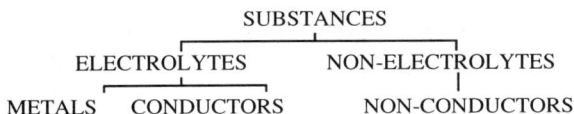

  B.

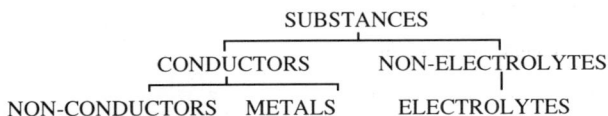

  C.

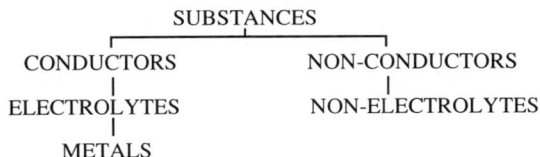

  D.

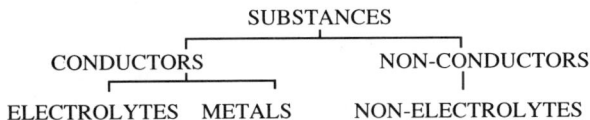

Test 7.5   Electron arrangement and ionic compounds

General /Credit level

Question 1 to 6 refer to the formation of ions.

      A.   atoms which gain electrons to form ions

      B.   atoms which lose electrons to form ions

      C.   atoms which do **not** readily form ions

Which statement is likely to apply to each of the following?

1.   an atom with 17 electrons

2.   an atom with 10 electrons

3.   an atom with 3 electrons

4.   an atom with 20 electrons

5.   an atom with 8 electrons

6.   an atom with 2 electrons

Questions 7 to 14 refer to the electron arrangements of atoms and ions.

Decide whether each of the following have

      A.   the **same** electron arrangement

      B.   a **different** electron arrangement.

7.   a magnesium atom and a neon atom

8.   a chloride ion and an argon atom

9.   an oxide ion an a sodium ion

10.   a potassium ion and a chlorine atom

11.   an aluminium ion and a fluoride ion

12.   a calcium ion and an oxide ion

13.   a lithium ion and a fluoride ion

14.   a sodium ion and a neon atom

Questions 15 to 20 refer to the formation of a calcium ion (Ca^{2+}).

Decide whether each of the following statements is

A. TRUE   **B.** FALSE.

15.   The number of protons increases by two.

16.   The number of neutrons remains the same.

17.   The number of electrons increases by two.

18.   The atomic number remains the same.

19.   The mass number decreases by two.

20.   The number of electrons decreases by two.

Questions 21 to 25 refer to neon, a gas which is used in lighting and advertising displays.

Decide whether each of the following statements is

A. TRUE   **B.** FALSE.

21.   An atom has the same electron arrangement as a Cl^- ion.

22.   An atom has two more electrons than an atom of oxygen.

23.   An atom has the same number of outer electrons as an atom of helium.

24.   An atom has a stable electron arrangement.

25.   An atom has the same number of electrons as an Al^{3+} ion.

Questions 26 to 30 refer to the reaction which occurs when a bromine atom gains one electron to from a bromide ion.

Decide whether each of the following statements is

A. TRUE   **B.** FALSE.

26.   The atomic number increases by one.

27.   The particle becomes negatively charged.

28.   The number of electron energy levels increases by one.

29.   The bromide ion has the same electron arrangement as an argon atom.

30.   The mass number increases by one.

31. A sodium atom and a sodium ion must have different numbers of

    A. protons, but the same number of electrons

    B. neutrons, but the same number of electrons

    C. electrons, but the same number of protons

    D. neutrons, but the same number of of protons.

32. A negatively charged particle with electron arrangment 2,8 could be a

    A. fluorine atom   **B.** fluoride ion

    C. sodium atom   **D.** sodium ion.

33. The particle with a two-positive charge and an electron arrangement 2,8,8 is

    A. calcium atom   **B.** magnesium atom

    C. calcium ion   **D.** magnesium ion.

34. A potassium ion has one more electron than

    A. an argon atom   **B.** a calcium ion

    C. a chlorine atom   **D.** a sulphide ion.

35. In which of the following compounds do both ions present have the electron arrangement of 2,8,8?

    A. sodium fluoride   **B.** lithium chloride

    C. potassium chloride   **D.** potassium fluoride

36. In which of the following compounds do both ions present have the same electron arrangement as the gas neon.

    A. sodium chloride   **B.** calcium fluoride

    C. sodium oxide   **D.** magnesium fluoride

Questions 37 to 43 refer to types of formulae for compounds in which **X** and **Y** are positive and negative ions respectively.

A.	**XY**	**B.**	**XY$_2$**	**C.**	**XY$_3$**
D.	**X$_2$Y**	**E.**	**X$_3$Y$_2$**		

Which is the type of formula for each of the following compounds?

37.   aluminium fluoride

38.   sodium oxide

39.   magnesium sulphide

40.   calcium fluoride

41.   lithium bromide

42.   magnesium nitride

43.   barium iodide

Questions 44 to 50 refer to the ratio of positive ions to negative ions in ionic compounds.

A.	one to one	**B.**	one to two	**C.**	two to one
D.	one to three	**E.**	three to one		

What is the ratio of positive ions to negative ions in each of the following compounds?

44. KNO_3

45. Na_2SO_4

46. Na_3PO_4

47. NH_4NO_3

48.   calcium nitrate

49.   ammonium chloride

50.   aluminium hydroxide

Properties of substances   57

General level

Questions 1 to 6 refer to the following colours of Universal indicator.

    A.   green   **B.**   red   **C.**   blue

Which could be colour of Universal indicator in each of the following solutions?

1.   acid solution

2.   alkaline solution

3.   neutral solution

4.   a solution with a pH of 7

5.   a solution with a pH of 2

6.   a solution with a pH of 10

In questions 7 to 14, decide whether each of the following statements about the pH of solutions is

    A. TRUE   **B.** FALSE.

7.   pH 4 is more acidic than pH 6.

8.   pH 8 is more alkaline that pH 10.

9.   pH 3 is less acidic than pH 1.

10.   pH 13 is more alkaline than pH 11.

11.   An acid can have a pH of 3.8.

12.   An alkali can have a pH value of 10.4.

11.   An acid can have a negative pH.

12.   An alkali can have a pH above 14.

Questions 13 to 16 refer to samples of rain water, taken as shown.

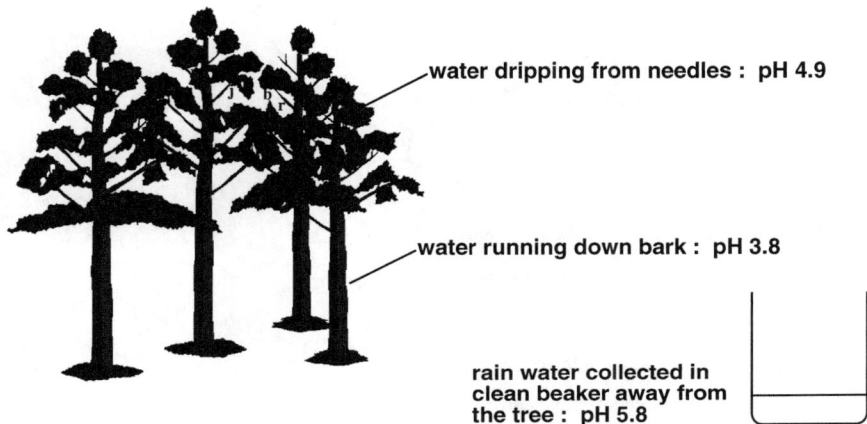

water dripping from needles : pH 4.9

water running down bark : pH 3.8

rain water collected in
clean beaker away from
the tree : pH 5.8

Decide whether each of the following statements is

    A. TRUE   **B.** FALSE.

13.   The rain water is acidic.

14.   The water running down the bark is less acidic than the water dripping from the needles.

15.   Pine bark has no effect on the acidity of rain water.

16.   Pine needles increase the acidity of rain water.

Acids and alkalis

Test 8.2 **Water**

General level

Decide whether each of the following statements about water is

    A. TRUE   **B.** FALSE.

1. Water has a pH of 8.

2. Water is mainly a covalent compound.

3. The concentration of ions in water is small.

4. Water is neutral to Universal indicator.

5. Water does **not** conduct electricity.

6. Water contains molecules of hydrogen oxide.

Question 7 to 10 refer to the effect of dilution on acids, alkalis, and neutral solutions.

Decide whether each of the following statements is

    A. TRUE   **B.** FALSE.

7. Diluting an alkali gives a more concentrated solution.

8. Diluting an acid increases the pH.

9. Diluting a neutral solution increases the pH.

10. Diluting an acid increases the acidity.

11. Diluting an alkali increases the pH.

12. Diluting a neutral solution does **not** change the pH.

Test 8.3 Oxides and hydroxides

General level

The questions in this test refer to types of oxides and hydroxides.

A. those which dissolve in water to give a solution of pH less than 7

B. those which dissolve in water to give a solution of pH greater than 7

C. those which have no effect on the pH of water

To which of the categories do each of the following oxides and hydroxides belong?

(You may wish to use the Data Booklet.)

1. sulphur dioxide
2. sodium oxide
3. carbon dioxide
4. copper(II) oxide
5. lithium hydroxide
6. calcium oxide
7. potassium oxide
8. iron(III) oxide
9. phosphorus oxide
10. copper(II) hydroxide
11. nitrogen dioxide
12. barium hydroxide

Test 8.4

The pH scale (ii)

Credit level

Questions 1 to 12 refer to the pH of solutions.

Decide whether each of the following statements is

  A. TRUE   **B.** FALSE.

1. A solution with pH 2 contains more $H^+(aq)$ than $OH^-(aq)$.

2. A solution with pH 6 contains a higher concentration of $H^+(aq)$ than a solution with pH 4.

3. A solution with pH 5 contains $H^+(aq)$ but **no** $OH^-(aq)$.

4. A solution with pH 7 contains an equal concentration of $H^+(aq)$ and $OH^-(aq)$.

5. A solution with pH 10 contains more $OH^-(aq)$ than $H^+(aq)$.

6. A solution with pH 11 contains **both** $OH^-(aq)$ and $H^+(aq)$.

7. A solution with pH 9 contains more $OH^-(aq)$ than pH 11.

8. A solution with pH 7 contains a higher concentration of $H^+(aq)$ than $OH^-(aq)$.

9. A solution with pH 6 contains an equal concentration of $H^+(aq)$ and $OH^-(aq)$.

10. A solution with pH 6 contains a higher concentration of $OH^-(aq)$ than pH 1.

11. A solution with pH 2 contains the same concentration of $OH^-(aq)$ ions as pure water.

12. A solution with pH 8 contains the same concentration of $H^+(aq)$ ions as pure water.

Questions 13 and 14 refer to the effect of dilution on acids and alkalis.

Decide whether each of the following statements is

  A. TRUE   **B.** FALSE.

13. As the concentration of $H^+(aq)$ ions in an acid increases, the pH of the solution increases.

14. As the concentration of $OH^-(aq)$ ions in an alkali decreases, the pH of the solution increases.

Test 9.1 Reactions of dilute acids

General level

Questions 1 to 3 refer to solutions of compounds with the following formulae.

A. KCl	**B.** HNO_3	**C.** HCl
D. NH_3	**E.** $(NH_4)_2SO_4$	**F.** H_2SO_4

1. What is the formula for hydrochloric acid?
2. What is the formula for nitric acid?
3. What is the formula for sulphuric acid?

Questions 4 to 6 refer to the following acids.

A. hydrochloric acid

B. sulphuric acid

C. nitric acid

4. What acid should be used in the reaction with alkali to prepare potassium sulphate?
5. What acid should be used in the reaction with alkali to prepare sodium chloride?
6. What acid should be used in the reaction with alkali to prepare lithium nitrate?

In questions 7 to 14, decide whether each of the following reactions

A. can be classified as a neutralisation reaction

B. can **NOT** be classified as a neutralisation reaction.

7. sodium chloride solution / silver nitrate solution
8. dilute hydrochloric acid / sodium hydroxide solid
9. calcium carbonate lumps / dilute nitric acid
10. magnesium / dilute sulphuric acid
11. potassium hydroxide solution / copper(II) chloride solution
12. copper(II) oxide solid / dilute hydrochloric acid
13. ammonium chloride solid / calcium hydroxide solid
14. dilute sulphuric acid / barium chloride solution

In questions 15 to 22, decide whether each of the following reactions

    A.   produces a salt and water **only**

    B.   produces a salt, water and carbon dioxide gas

    C.   produces a salt and hydrogen.

15. magnesium carbonate with sulphuric acid

16. copper(II) oxide with sulphuric acid

17. zinc with sulphuric acid

18. sodium hydroxide with nitric acid

19. calcium carbonate with hydrochloric acid

20. barium oxide with nitric acid

21. magnesium with hydrochloric acid

22. potassium hydroxide with hydrochloric acid

General level

The questions in this test refer to the mixing of pairs of solutions.

Decide whether

    A.   a precipitate is formed

    B.   a precipitate is **NOT** formed.

(You may wish to use the Data Booklet.)

1.   sodium chloride and potassium nitrate

2.   potassium sulphate and barium chloride

3.   lead(II) nitrate and sodium sulphate

4.   calcium chloride and potassium nitrate

5.   sodium nitrate and copper(II) sulphate

6.   magnesium chloride and calcium nitrate

7.   silver nitrate and potassium chloride

8.   ammonium chloride and sodium nitrate

9.   lead(II) nitrate and sodium carbonate

10.   potassium sulphate and copper(II) nitrate

Credit level

In questions 1 to 12, decide whether each of the following compounds

    A. can be classified as a salt

    B. can **NOT** be classified as a salt.

1.	magnesium oxide	7.	hydrogen sulphide
2.	potassium chloride	8.	lithium sulphate
3.	calcium hydroxide	9.	nitrogen chloride
4.	hydrogen chloride	10.	magnesium nitride
5.	sodium sulphate	11.	ammonium sulphate
6.	copper nitrate	12.	silicon oxide

Questions 13 to 20 refer to the preparation of salts by the following methods.

    A. precipitation

    B. reaction of acid with alkali

    C. reaction of acid with insoluble metal oxide

Which method is most suitable for the preparation of the following salts?

(You may wish to use the Data Booklet.)

13.	potassium chloride	17.	barium sulphate
14.	lead(II) sulphate	18.	magnesium nitrate
15.	iron(III) sulphate	19.	copper(II) chloride
16.	silver chloride	20.	sodium nitrate

Test 9.4   Bases

Credit level

In questions 1 to 10, decide whether each of the following metal compounds

    A. can be classified as a base

    B. can **NOT** be classified as a base.

(You may wish to use the Data Booklet.)

1.   sodium hydroxide

2.   potassium nitrate

3.   copper(II) oxide

4.   calcium chloride

5.   calcium oxide

6.   magnesium sulphate

7.   lead(II) carbonate

8.   potassium hydroxide

9.   sodium chloride

10.   barium oxide

In questions 11 to 20, decide whether each of the following metal compounds

    A. reacts with water to form an alkali

    B. does **NOT** react with water to form an alkali.

(You may wish to use the Data Booklet.)

11.   copper(II) nitrate

12.   potassium oxide

13.   iron(III) hydroxide

14.   barium sulphate

15.   copper(II) hydroxide

16.   sodium chloride

17.   lithium hydroxide

18.   lead(II) chloride

19.   barium hydroxide

20.   zinc oxide

General / Credit level

Questions 1 to 10 refer to the direction of electron flow in the apparatus shown.

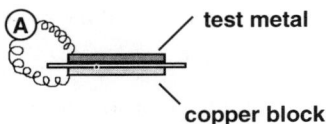

test metal

copper block

Which is the direction of electron flow when each of the following pairs of test metals are attached?

1.	**A.**	magnesium to copper.	**B.**	copper to magnesium
2.	**A.**	magnesium to iron	**B.**	iron to magnesium
3.	**A.**	magnesium to silver	**B.**	silver to magnesium
4.	**A.**	magnesium to sodium	**B.**	sodium to magnesium
5.	**A.**	iron to copper	**B.**	copper to iron
6.	**A.**	iron to silver	**B.**	silver to iron
7.	**A.**	iron to sodium	**B.**	sodium to iron
8.	**A.**	silver to copper	**B.**	copper to silver
9.	**A.**	silver to sodium	**B.**	sodium to silver
10.	**A.**	tin to copper	**B.**	copper to tin

Question 11 and 12 refer to the apparatus shown.

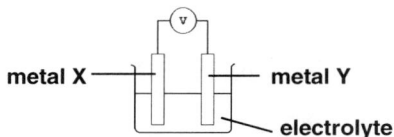

metal X

metal Y

electrolyte

11. Which of the following pairs of metals would give the largest reading on the voltmeter?

    A. iron / zinc   **B.** silver / magnesium

    C. zinc / copper   **D.** lead / copper

12. If the voltmeter was replaced by an ammeter which pair of metals would give an electron flow from metal **X** to metal **Y**.

	X	**Y**
A.	zinc	copper
B.	zinc	magnesium
C.	iron	zinc
D.	lead	iron

13. In the apparatus shown below the bulb will become brighter if the copper is replaced by

A. magnesium

B. lead

C. zinc

D. gold.

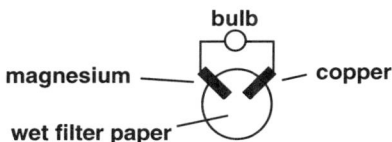

Questions 14 to 17 refer to the following results, which were obtained using the apparatus shown below.

Test metal	Voltmeter reading / V
magnesium	1.6
iron	0.5
silver	-0.4
tin	0.4
sodium	2.4

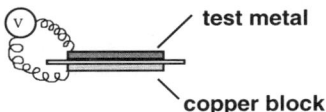

14. Which of the metals used in the experiment is best at supplying electrons?

A. silver   B. iron   C. sodium   D. magnesium

15. Which of the metals used in the experiment is poorest at supplying electrons?

A. copper   B. sodium   C. silver   D. magnesium

16. If the copper block was replaced by a test metal, which of the following pairs of metals would give the largest reading on the voltmeter?

A. silver and tin   B. magnesium and tin

C. silver and sodium   D. magnesium and sodium

17. If the copper block was replaced by a block of tin, which metal could be used as the test metal to give a voltmeter reading of approximately 1.2 V?

A. magnesium   B. iron   C. sodium   D. silver

Making electricity

Questions 18 and 19 refer to the apparatus shown.

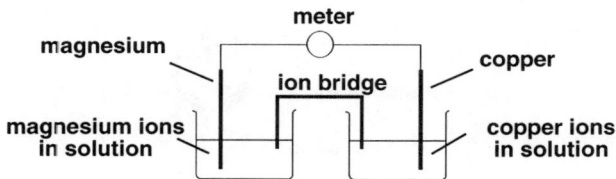

18.   Electrons flow from

   A.   magnesium to copper through the meter

   B.   copper to magnesium through the meter

   C.   magnesium to copper through the ion bridge

   D.   copper to magnesium through the ion bridge.

19.   Which of the following metals/metal ions can replace the magnesium/magnesium ions and produce a flow of electrons in the opposite direction?

   A.   zinc   **B.**   gold   **C.**   iron   **D.**   lead

In questions 20 to 25, decide whether aqueous solutions of each of the following

   A. can be used as an electrolyte

   B. can **NOT** be used as an electrolyte.

20.   sodium chloride

21.   sucrose $(C_{12}H_{22}O_{11})$

22.   ethanol (C_2H_5OH)

23.   ammonium sulphate

24.   glucose $(C_6H_{12}O_6)$

25.   potassium nitrate

Credit level

The questions in this test refer to the addition of a metal to a solution containing ions.

In each case decide whether a reaction

    A. takes place

    B. does **NOT** take place.

(You may wish to use the Data Booklet.)

1.   copper added to silver nitrate solution

2.   magnesium added to sodium sulphate solution

3.   iron added to dilute hydrochloric acid

4.   zinc added to copper(II) sulphate solution

5.   silver added to potassium chloride solution

6.   copper added to dilute sulphuric acid

7.   tin added to magnesium nitrate solution

8.   silver added to dilute hydrochloric acid

9.   iron added to copper(II) nitrate solution

10.   magnesium added to dilute sulphuric acid

Test 10.3

Oxidation and reduction

Credit level

Decide whether each of the following reactions involve

    A. oxidation   **B.** reduction.

(You may wish to use the Data Booklet.)

1. $Zn^{2+}(aq) + 2e^- \rightarrow Zn(s)$

2. $Ag(s) \rightarrow Ag^+(aq) + e^-$

3. $Br_2(l) + 2e^- \rightarrow 2Br^-(aq)$

4. $Sn^{2+}(aq) + 2e^- \rightarrow Sn(s)$

5. $2Cl^-(aq) \rightarrow Cl_2(g)$

6. $Mg^{2+}(aq) \rightarrow Mg(s)$

7. $Fe(s) \rightarrow Fe^{2+}(aq)$

8. $SO_3^{2-}(aq) \rightarrow SO_4^{2-}(aq)$

9. nickel(III) $\rightarrow$ nickel(II)

10. cobalt(II) $\rightarrow$ cobalt (III)

11. copper atoms $\rightarrow$ copper ions

12. iodine molecules $\rightarrow$ iodide ions.

Credit level

Decide whether each of the following is

    A. a redox reaction   **B.** **NOT** a redox reaction.

1. $Zn(s)$ + $2H^+(aq)$ $\rightarrow$ $Zn^{2+}(aq)$ + $H_2(g)$

2. $OH^-(aq)$ + $H^+(aq)$ $\rightarrow$ $H_2O(l)$

3. $Mg(s)$ + $Cu^{2+}(aq)$ $\rightarrow$ $Mg^{2+}(aq)$ + $Cu(s)$

4. $Ag^+(aq)$ + $Cl^-(aq)$ $\rightarrow$ $AgCl(s)$

5. $Cl_2(g)$ + $2I^-(aq)$ $\rightarrow$ $2Cl^-(aq)$ + $I_2(aq)$

6. $NH_4^+(aq)$ + $OH^-(aq)$ $\rightarrow$ $NH_3(g)$ + $H_2O(l)$

7. $SO_3^{2-}(aq)$ + $H_2O(l)$ + $Br_2(l)$ $\rightarrow$ $SO_4^{2-}(aq)$ + $2H^+(aq)$ + $2Br^-(aq)$

8. $SnCl_2(aq)$ + $HgCl_2$ $\rightarrow$ $Hg(l)$ + $SnCl_4(aq)$

9. $C_2H_4(g)$ + $Br_2(g)$ $\rightarrow$ $C_2H_4Br_2(l)$

10. $2FeO(s)$ + $C(s)$ $\rightarrow$ $2Fe(s)$ + $CO_2(g)$

11. $2Mg(s)$ + $O_2(g)$ $\rightarrow$ $2\,MgO(s)$

12. $Na_2SO_4(aq)$ + $BaCl_2(aq)$ $\rightarrow$ $2NaCl(aq)$ + $BaSO_4(s)$

13. $CuO(s)$ + $2HNO_3(aq)$ $\rightarrow$ $Cu(NO_3)_2(aq)$ + $H_2O(l)$

14. $F_2(g))$ + $NaBr(aq)$ $\rightarrow$ $Br_2(aq)$ + $2NaF(aq)$

15. $CaCO_3(s)$ $\rightarrow$ $CaO(s)$ + $CO_2(g)$

16. $2Na_2S_2O_3(aq)$ + $I_2(aq)$ $\rightarrow$ $2NaI(aq)$ + $Na_2S_4O_6(aq)$

17. $2Na(s)$ + $2H_2O(l)$ $\rightarrow$ $2NaOH(aq)$ + $H_2(g)$

18. $2Fe(NO_3)_3(aq)$ + $2KI(aq)$ $\rightarrow$ $2Fe(NO_3)_2(aq)$ + $2KNO_3(aq)$ + $I_2(aq)$

Test 10.5 Electrolysis (ii)

Credit level

Questions 1 to 6 refer to what happens at the negative electrode during the electrolysis of lead iodide melt.

Decide whether each of the following statements is

A. TRUE **B.** FALSE.

1. lead metal appears
2. iodide ions are reduced
3. lead atoms are reduced
4. lead ions are reduced
5. lead ions are oxidised
6. iodide ions are oxidised

Questions 7 to 12 refer to what happens at the positive electrode during the electrolysis of copper chloride solution.

Decide whether each of the following statements is

A. TRUE **B.** FALSE.

7. copper metal is formed
8. chlorine is formed
9. copper ions are reduced
10. chloride ions are reduced
11. chloride ions are oxidised
12. chlorine atoms are oxidised

13. The experiment opposite shows how a piece of copper can be nickel-plated.

Which of the reactions below is taking place at the negative electrode?

A. nickel ions are being reduced

B. nickel ions are being oxidised

C. nickel atoms are being oxidised

D. nickel atoms are being reduced

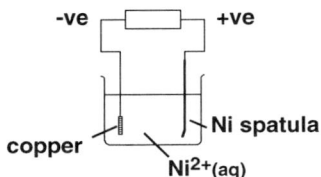

Questions 14 to 16 refer to the experiment opposite which shows how copper can be purified.

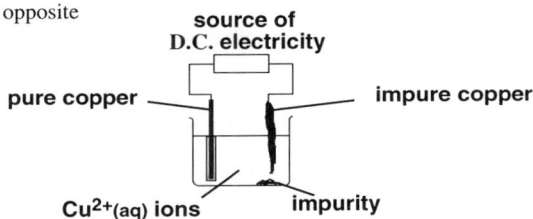

14. The impure copper is attached to which terminal of the battery?

A. negative   B. positive

15. Which reaction takes place at the pure copper electrode?

A. copper ions are being reduced

B. copper ions are being oxidised

C. copper atoms are being oxidised

D. copper atoms are being reduced

16. Which reaction takes place at the impure copper electrode?

A. copper ions are being reduced

B. copper ions are being oxidised

C. copper atoms are being oxidised

D. copper atoms are being reduced

Questions 17 to 20 refer to the purification of copper by the following electrolysis process.

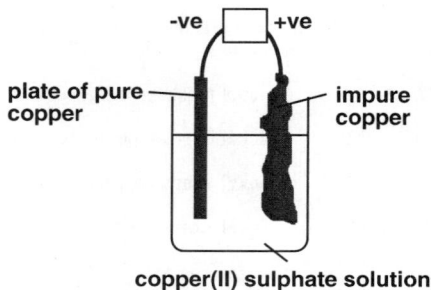

copper(II) sulphate solution

The impure copper forms copper ions in solution.

Decide whether each of the following statements is

    A. TRUE   **B.** FALSE.

17.   The pure copper plate increases in mass.

18.   The solution becomes colourless.

19.   The copper(II) ions are reduced.

20.   The pure copper plate is oxidised.

Questions 21 to 24 refer to a process which can be used to coat a metal fork with a layer of nickel.

The following apparatus is used in the process.

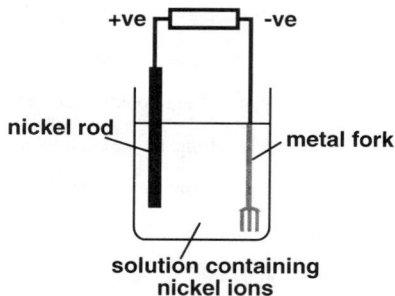

solution containing nickel ions

Decide whether each of the following statements is

    A. TRUE   **B.** FALSE.

21.   Electrons move through the solution.

22.   The nickel ions move towards the nickel rod.

23.   Oxidation occurs at the nickel rod.

24.   The process is an example of electroplating.

25.   The mass of the nickel rod increases.

General level

Questions 1 to 4 refer to reactions of the following metals.

    A. gold   **B.** sodium

    C. magnesium   **D.** copper

1. Which metal combines with the oxygen of the air and reacts vigorously with water?

2. Which metal reacts with the oxygen of the air when heated but does **not** react with water?

3. Which metal does **not** react with the oxygen of the air and does **not** react with water?

4. Which metal reacts vigorously with the oxygen of the air when heated and reacts slowly with water?

In questions 5 to 10, decide whether each of the following metals

    A. reacts with dilute acid

    B. does **NOT** react with dilute acid.

5.	copper	8.	zinc
6.	magnesium	9.	gold
7.	iron	10.	silver

In questions 11 to 16, decide whether each of the following metals

    A. is found uncombined in the Earth's crust

    B. is **always** found as ores.

11.	silver	14.	sodium
12.	iron	15.	gold
13.	copper	16.	aluminium

Questions 17 to 19 refer to the metals listed below.

    A.   calcium   **B.**   lithium   **C.**   silver   **D.**   zinc

17.   Which metal must be stored under oil?

18.   Which metal safely reacts with water, allowing the gas given off to be safely collected?

19.   Which metal does **not** react with water but reacts with dilute acid?

20.   When two metals were added to (i) cold water and (ii) dilute acid, no difference in activity was observed.

The metals could have been

    A. zinc and calcium   **B.** silver and copper

    C. lead and magnesium   **D.** iron and gold.

21.   The reaction in the apparatus shown below is used to provide the gas to inflate the balloon.

Which of the following metals is the most suitable to use?

    A.   copper   **B.**   sodium   **C.**   magnesium   **D.**   silver

Questions 22 and 28 refer to the dates of discovery of metals.

Decide whether each of the following metals was

    A. discovered in the nineteenth century

    B. discovered **before** the nineteenth century.

22.   aluminium

23.   gold

24.   copper

25.   tin

26.   calcium

27.   sodium

28.   iron

Test 11.2 Stability of metal oxides

General level

Questions 1 to 4 refer to the heating of metal oxides.

Decide whether each of the following metal oxides

A. breaks up to give the metal **B.** does **NOT** break up.

1. sodium oxide
2. silver oxide
3. copper oxide
4. mercury oxide

Questions 5 to 10 refer to the heating of metal oxides with carbon.

Decide whether each of the following metal oxides

A. breaks up to give the metal **B.** does **NOT** break up.

5. calcium oxide
6. magnesium oxide
7. lead oxide
8. copper oxide
9. sodium oxide
10. iron oxide

Test 11.3

General level

The reactivity series (ii)

1. An unknown metal was found to be more reactive than sodium.

   Which of the following predictions about the metal is likely to be correct?

   A. It will react readily with the oxygen of the air.

   B. It should be stored under water.

   C. Its compounds will be unstable.

   D. It will be obtained from its oxide by heating with carbon.

2. Sodium is a very reactive metal.

   Which of the following would be expected to produce sodium?

   A. passing electricity through molten sodium chloride

   B. heating sodium oxide in air

   C. heating sodium oxide with carbon

3. An unknown metal was found uncombined in the Earth's crust.

   Which of the following predictions about the metal is likely to be correct?

   A. It will be stored under oil.

   B. Its compounds will be stable.

   C. It will react with dilute acid.

   D. Its oxide will decompose on heating.

4. Iron(II) oxide can be broken up by heating with carbon, but barium oxide is unaffected by this treatment.

   Which of the following statements can be deduced from these facts?

   A. Iron is a more reactive metal than barium.

   B. Oxides of metals are stable compounds.

   C. Barium ions form atoms less easily than do iron(II) ions.

5.   The following facts are known about four metals, **P, Q , R**, and **S**.

(i)   **R** displaces **P** and **S** from solutions of their ions;
(ii) **Q** reacts with water, **R** does not;
(iii) only the oxide of metal **S** can be decomposed to give metal.

The order of reactivity (most reactive first) is

A. **R, Q, S, P**   B. **Q, S, P, R**

C. **P, S, Q, R**   D. **Q, R, P, S**.

6.   A metallic element reacts with dilute hydrochloric acid releasing hydrogen. The oxide of the metal can be decomposed by heating with carbon.

From this information alone the position of the metal in the reactivity series could be between

A. silver and copper   B. zinc and tin

B. magnesium and sodium   D. calcium and aluminium.

7.   The following information relates to four metals, **W, X, Y,** and **Z**.

(i)   **W** displaces **X** from a solution of its compound;
(ii) only **Z** is stored under oil;
(iii) only the oxide of metal **Y** releases oxygen on heating.

The order of reactivity (most reactive first) is

A. **Y, W, X, Z**   B. **Z, W, X, Y**

C. **Z, X, W, Y**   D. **Y, X, W, Z**.

General / Cedit level

Questions 1 and 2 refer to the diagram below.

The diagram shows an experiment set up to investigate the corrosion of iron.

The water level inside the tube rises as corrosion takes place.

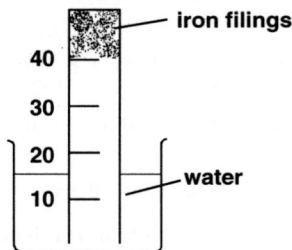

1. Which gas in the air is reacting with the iron?

    A. nitrogen   **B.** oxygen

    C. carbon dioxide   **D.** none of these

2. What will be the approximate final level of the water?

    A. 10   **B.** 20   **C.** 30   **D.** 40

3. The corrosion of which metal is called rusting?

    A. copper   **B.** silver

    C. tin   **D.** iron

4. Which of the following solutions is used to show the extent of the rusting process?

    A. Universal indicator   **B.** lime water

    C. ferroxyl indicator   **D.** bromine solution

Questions 5 to 9 refer to experiments which are set up to investigate the speed of rusting.
In each of the following cases, decide in which experiment the iron nail will rust faster.

5. A.   B.

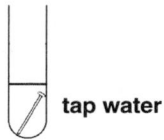 tap water    oil film
                                                 boiled water

6. A.   B.

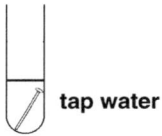 tap water    drying agent

7. A.   B.

 tap water    sea water

8. A.   B.

 tap water   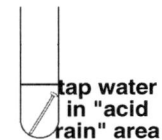 tap water
                                                 in "acid
                                                 rain" area

9. A.   B.

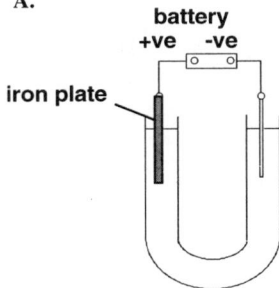   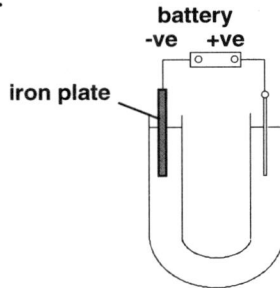

Questions 10 to 15 refer to the attaching of different metals to an iron nail.

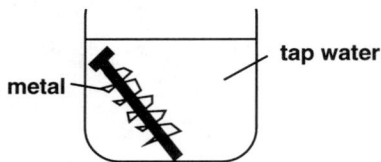

Decide whether each of the following metals

    A.   protects the iron from corrosion

    B.   does **NOT** protect the iron from corrosion.

10.   tin

11.   magnesium

12.   silver

13.   copper

14.   zinc

15.   lead

Questions 16 to 18 refer to the following methods for protecting iron from corrosion.

    A.   electroplating   **B.**   galvanising   **C.**   sacrificial protection

16.   What name is given to the process in which iron is dipped into molten zinc to give it a protective layer?

17.   What name is given to the process in which scrap magnesium is used to protect an iron structure?

18.   What name is given to the process in which electrolysis is used to coat iron with another metal?

19.   Corrosion of iron can be prevented by putting a barrier of another metal between the iron and the atmosphere.

    A coating of which metal will lead to sacrificial protection if the barrier is broken?

    A.   copper   **B.**   silver   **C.**   tin   **D.**   zinc

20.   Small metal plates can be fixed to the iron chassis of a car to reduce corrosion.

    These plates could be made of

    A.   tin   **B.**   calcium   **C.**   magnesium   **D.**   copper.

21.   In which of the following situations is sacrificial corrosion useful?

    A.   iron cans plated with tin

    B.   iron plates riveted with copper rivets

    C.   steel ships fitted with zinc below the water line

    D.   lead connected to iron pipes

Questions 22 to 25 refer to the riveting of metal plates.

Riveted metal plates can loosen due to corrosion of the metal rivets.

In each of the following cases, decide whether

    A.   the plates corrode before the rivets

    B.   the rivets corrode before the plates.

22.   copper plates and iron rivets

23.   zinc plates and aluminium rivets

24.   silver plates with copper rivets

25.   iron plates and copper rivets

26.   When a cell is set up with iron and an unknown metal **X**, the electron flow in the external circuit is from iron to **X**.

    Which of the following statements is a correct deduction from this observation?

    A.   It will be possible to use metal **X** for the sacrificial protection of iron.

    B.   Corrosion of metal **X** in air is likely to be rapid.

    C.   An iron container coated with metal **X**   will not corrode even when the coating is broken.

    D.   It will be unwise to use rivets made of metal **X** in an iron structure.

27.   Galvanising and tin-plating are two methods of protecting iron from corrosion. They work equally well until the protective layer is broken.

    The galvanised iron then lasts longer because

    A.   galvanising gives thicker plating than tin plating

    B.   zinc is higher in the reactivity series than iron

    C.   tin is higher in the reactivity series than zinc

    D.   galvanising increases the thickness of the oxide coat on the iron.

Credit level

1. During corrosion, the reaction involving the metal is an example of

   A. oxidation   **B.** reduction.

Questions 2 to 7 refer to the diagram opposite.

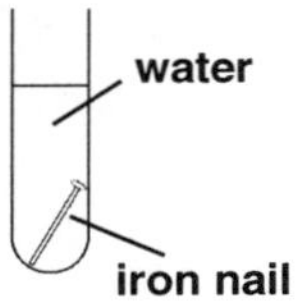

Decide whether each of the following substances, when added to the water, would

   A. be expected to increase the speed of rusting

   B. **NOT** be expected to increase the speed of rusting.

2. carbon dioxide   5. sucrose

3. starch   6. salt

4. potassium nitrate   7. calcium carbonate

Questions 8 to 10 refer to cells with an iron nail as one of the electrodes.

The iron nail is immersed in a gel with ferroxyl indicator and an electrolyte.

8. In the cell shown opposite, a blue colour will appear at

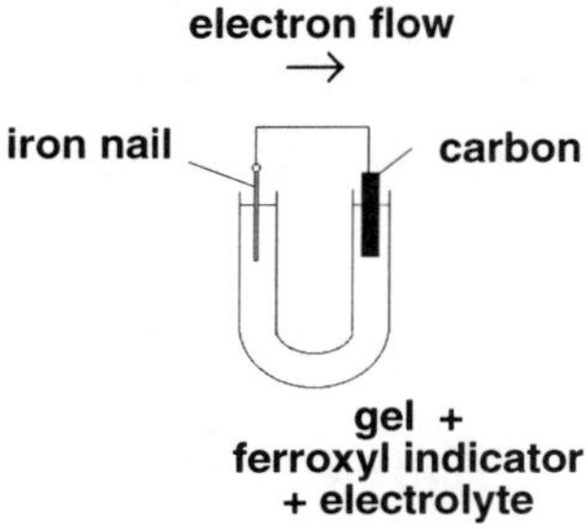

   A. the carbon rod

   B. the iron nail

   C. **neither** the carbon rod **nor** the iron nail

   D. **both** the carbon rod **and** the iron nail.

9. In the cell shown opposite, a blue colour will appear at

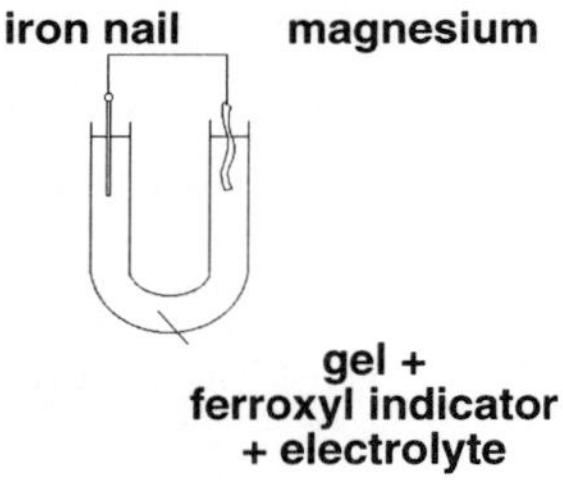

   A. the magnesium ribbon

   B. the iron nail

   C. **neither** the magnesium ribbon **nor** the iron nail

   D. **both** the magnesium ribbon **and** the iron nail

10. In the cell shown opposite, a blue colour will appear at

   A. the copper foil

   B. the iron nail

   C. **neither** the copper foil
      nor the iron nail

   D. **both** the copper foil
      and the iron nail.

iron nail   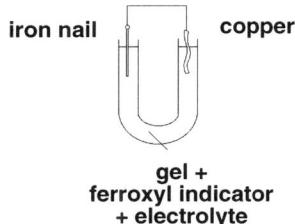   **copper**

gel +
ferroxyl indicator
+ electrolyte

Questions 11 to 15 refer to the protection of iron from rusting.

Decide whether each of the following statements is

   A. TRUE   **B.** FALSE.

11. Copper gives sacrificial protection to iron.

12. Ferroxyl indicator turns pink in the presence of Fe^{2+} ions.

13. Electroplating provides a surface barrier to air and water.

14. Tin plated iron rusts quickly when the coating is scratched.

15. Iron rusts faster when attached to the negative terminal of a battery.

Questions 16 to 21 refer to an iron gate which has been galvanised, i.e. coated with zinc.

The gate has been scratched to expose the iron.

Decide whether each of the following statements is

   A. TRUE   **B.** FALSE.

16. The zinc increases the rate of corrosion of iron.

17. The zinc is oxidised.

18. The zinc attracts electrons from the iron.

18. The zinc does **not** corrode.

20. The zinc corrodes slower than the iron.

21. The zinc is sacrificed to protect the iron.

Questions 22 to 26 refer to a gas pipeline made from iron which is protected by attaching scrap magnesium.

Decide whether each of the following statements is

      A. TRUE   **B.** FALSE.

22.   The magnesium is oxidised.

23.   The magnesium does **not** corrode.

24.   The iron corrodes faster than the magnesium.

25.   The magnesium provides sacrificial protection.

26.   Electrons flow from the iron to the magnesium.

Questions 27 to 32 refer to the following experiment.

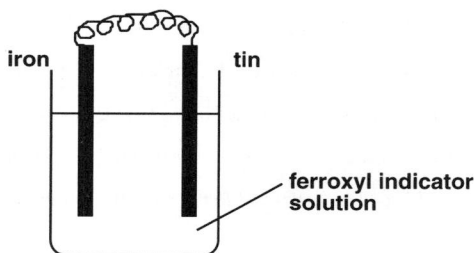

Decide whether each of the following statements is

      A. TRUE   **B.** FALSE.

27.   Tin atoms are oxidised.

28.   Iron ions are reduced.

29.   A blue colour forms around the iron.

30.   The mass of iron decreases.

31.   The electrons flow through the wire from the tin.

32.   A pink colour forms around the tin.

General level

Decide whether each of the following statements is

    A. TRUE   **B.** FALSE.

1. Plastics are good conductors of heat.

2. Many fibres are made from oil.

3. Most plastics are biodegradable.

4. Some plastics burn or smoulder to give off toxic fumes.

5. A thermoplastic melts on heating.

6. Plastics are examples of electrical insulators.

7. Plastics are examples of monomers.

8. Plastics are made from saturated molecules.

9. Polythene is a plastic made from ethene.

10. Many plastics are made from molecules produced by the cracking of hydrocarbons.

11. A thermosetting plastic can be easily reshaped.

12. Styrene is an example of a polymer.

13. Many plastics are made from methane (natural gas).

14. The making of plastics is an example of polymerisation.

15. Fibres are examples of polymers.

16. Many plastics are formed from alkenes.

17. Polystyrene is a plastic made from propene.

18.
$$-\overset{\overset{\displaystyle H}{|}}{\underset{\underset{\displaystyle H}{|}}{C}}-\overset{\overset{\displaystyle H}{|}}{\underset{\underset{\displaystyle H}{|}}{C}}-\overset{\overset{\displaystyle H}{|}}{\underset{\underset{\displaystyle H}{|}}{C}}-\overset{\overset{\displaystyle H}{|}}{\underset{\underset{\displaystyle H}{|}}{C}}-$$
is part of a poly(ethene) chain.

19. Polystyrene can be used for packaging because it is light.

20. The long chain in poly(propene) has many carbon to carbon double bonds.

21. A natural fibre is one which is made by the chemical industry.

22. Butene is a monomer used to make poly(butene).

General level

In questions 1 to 4, decide whether each of the following fibres is

    A. natural   **B.** synthetic.

1.   nylon   3.   cotton

2.   wool   4.   terylene

In questions 5 to 10, decide whether each of the following polymers is

    A. a thermosetting plastic   **B.** a thermoplastic.

5.   polystyrene   8.   polythene

6.   nylon   9.   bakelite

7.   formica   10.   poly(propene)

In questions 11 to 22, decide whether each of the following molecules is

    A. able to undergo polymerisation

    B. NOT able to undergo polymerisation.

11.

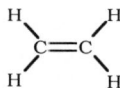

12.

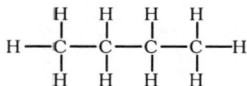

13.

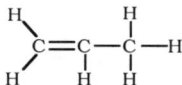

14.

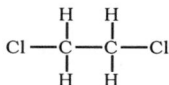

15.   ethane

16.   butene

17.   octane

18.   methylpropene

19. CH_4

20. C_2F_4

21. $C_2H_4Br_2$

22. C_3H_5Cl (straight-chain)

Credit level

Questions 1 to 4 refer to the burning or smouldering of some plastics.

Decide whether each of the following toxic gases could be produced.

    A.   carbon monoxide   **B.**   hydrogen chloride   **C.**   hydrogen cyanide

(Note that for some questions, more than one response may be correct.)

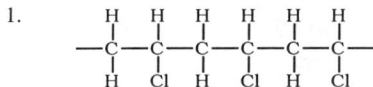

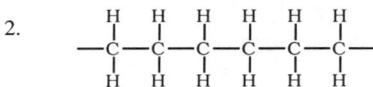

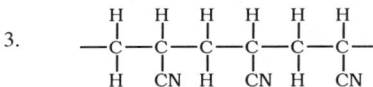

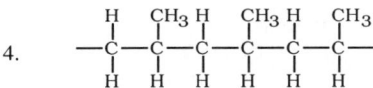

1.
```
    H    H    H    H    H    H
    |    |    |    |    |    |
  —C —— C —— C —— C —— C —— C—
    |    |    |    |    |    |
    H   Cl    H   Cl    H   Cl
```

2.
```
    H    H    H    H    H    H
    |    |    |    |    |    |
  —C —— C —— C —— C —— C —— C—
    |    |    |    |    |    |
    H    H    H    H    H    H
```

3.
```
    H    H    H    H    H    H
    |    |    |    |    |    |
  —C —— C —— C —— C —— C —— C—
    |    |    |    |    |    |
    H   CN    H   CN    H   CN
```

4.
```
    H   CH3   H   CH3   H   CH3
    |    |    |    |    |    |
  —C —— C —— C —— C —— C —— C—
    |    |    |    |    |    |
    H    H    H    H    H    H
```

Questions 5 to 8 refer to the part of the polymer shown below.

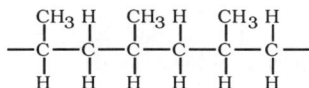

$$
\begin{array}{ccccccc}
 & CH_3 & H & CH_3 & H & CH_3 & H \\
 & | & | & | & | & | & | \\
-C & -C & -C & -C & -C & -C- \\
 & | & | & | & | & | & | \\
 & H & H & H & H & H & H
\end{array}
$$

5. How many repeating units are shown?

    A. 2   **B.** 3   **C.** 6   **D.** 9

6. What is the repeating unit?

    A.
$$
\begin{array}{cc}
H & H \\
| & | \\
-C-C- \\
| & | \\
H & H
\end{array}
$$

    B.
$$
\begin{array}{cc}
CH_3 & H \\
| & | \\
-C-C- \\
| & | \\
H & H
\end{array}
$$

    C.
$$
\begin{array}{cc}
CH_3 & H \\
| & | \\
C=C \\
| & | \\
H & H
\end{array}
$$

    D.
$$
\begin{array}{ccc}
H & CH_3 & H \\
| & | & | \\
-C-C-C- \\
| & | & | \\
H & H & H
\end{array}
$$

7. What is the name of the monomer?

    A. ethene   **B.** propane

    C. propene   **D.** butane

8. What is the name of the polymer?

    A. polythene   **B.** poly(propene)

    C. poly(butene)   **D.** P.V.C.

9. Polyvinyl chloride is a polymer of vinyl chloride, $CH_2=CHCl$ (chloroethene).

    Which of the following is part of the formula for polyvinyl chloride?

    A.
$$
\begin{array}{cccc}
Cl & Cl & Cl & Cl \\
| & | & | & | \\
-C-C-C-C- \\
| & | & | & | \\
H & H & H & H
\end{array}
$$

    B.
$$
\begin{array}{cccc}
H & Cl & H & Cl \\
| & | & | & | \\
-C-C-C-C- \\
| & | & | & | \\
Cl & H & Cl & H
\end{array}
$$

    C.
$$
\begin{array}{cccc}
H & Cl & H & Cl \\
| & | & | & | \\
-C-C-C-C- \\
| & | & | & | \\
H & H & H & H
\end{array}
$$

    D.
$$
\begin{array}{cccc}
H & Cl & H & Cl \\
| & | & | & | \\
-C=C-C=C- \\
\end{array}
$$

10. Acrilan is an addition polymer made from acrylonitrile. The structural formula for acrylonitrile is:

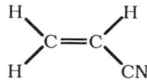

Which of the following is part of the structure of Acrilan?

A.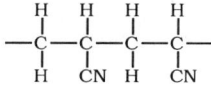

B.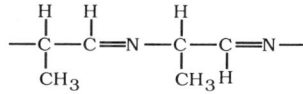

C.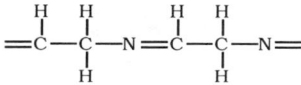

D.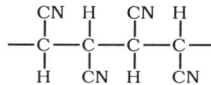

11.

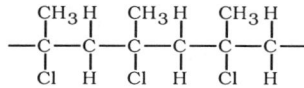

Which of the following monomers could polymerise to give the above polymer?

A.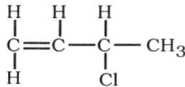

B.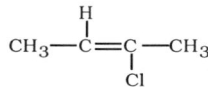

C.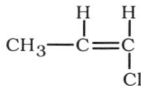

D.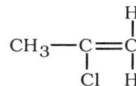

Test 14.1

General level

Decide whether each of the following statements is

    A. TRUE   **B.** FALSE.

1. The increasing world population has led to a need for more efficient food production.

2. Fertilisers can restore the essential elements for plant growth to the soil.

3. A good fertiliser is a substance which is insoluble in water.

4. Bacteria in the root nodules of some plants can convert atmospheric oxygen into oxygen compounds.

5. Ammonium compounds are useful fertilisers.

6. Animal manure is an example of a synthetic fertiliser.

7. Town sewage can be treated to produce fertiliser.

8. Potatoes and turnips can make nitrogen compounds from nitrogen in the air.

9. Compost can be useful to replace nitrogen compounds in the soil.

10. The eating of plants by animals is a step in the nitrogen cycle.

11. The leaves of some plants contain bacteria which build up nitrogen compounds from nitrogen in the air.

12. Potassium compounds contain an element required for healthy plant growth.

13. Essential nutrients are taken in by the roots of plants, as compounds dissolved in water.

14. Plants in the pea family are useful in increasing the fertility of the soil.

15. The Haber Process is important in the industrial manufacture of fertilisers.

16. The healthy growth of plants requires nutrients, including compounds of nitrogen, phosphorus and potassium.

17. Over-use of synthetic fertilisers can cause environmental problems.

18. Natural fertilisers are made by industrial processes.

19. Fertilisers are used to replace nitrogen which is lost from the nitrogen cycle.

20. Nitrogen oxides in rain water can increase the fertility of the soil.

21. Sodium chloride is a better fertiliser than potassium nitrate.

22. Nitric acid is used to make fertilisers.

23. Ammonia is used to make fertilisers.

24. In times of heavy rain, fertilisers can be washed out of the soil.

Test 14.2   The industrial manufacture of ammonia

General level

Decide whether each of the following statements about the industrial manufacture of ammonia is

    A. TRUE   **B.** FALSE.

1. Ammonia is made in industry from nitrogen and water.
2. The reaction is likely to be carried out at a very low temperature.
3. The catalyst speeds up the formation of ammonia.
4. The reaction is named the Haber Process.
5. An iron catalyst is used in the reaction.
6. Ammonia gas is cooled to remove it from the unchanged reactants.
7. The nitrogen for the reaction is obtained from nitrogen oxides.
8. The gases in the reaction chamber are kept at low pressure.
9. The catalyst is used to prevent the ammonia decomposing.
10. One of the reactants is obtained from methane (natural gas).
11. All the reactants are converted to ammonia.
12. Ammonia is produced from nitrogen and hydrogen.
13. The catalyst is used up in the reaction.
14. The word equation for the reaction is:

    nitrogen oxide + hydrogen → ammonia + oxygen
15. The unchanged reactants can be recycled.
16. The catalyst provides the surface on which the reaction takes place.
17. Ammonia is used to make fertilisers.
18. The nitrogen for the reaction is obtained by fractional distillation of liquid air.

General level

Decide whether each of the following statements about ammonia is

    A. TRUE   **B.** FALSE.

1. It turns damp pH paper red.

2. It does **not** have a smell.

3. It is insoluble in water.

4. It can be easily liquified.

5. It is a colourless gas.

6. It dissolves in water to form an alkali.

7. It can be converted to ammonium compounds.

8. It forms ammonium ions in solution.

General level

Decide whether each of the following statements is

      A. TRUE   **B.** FALSE.

1.   Nitrogen is constantly combining with the oxygen in the air.

2.   An acid is formed when nitrogen dioxide dissolves in water.

3.   A spark provides the energy for nitrogen dioxide to be produced from air in the laboratory.

4.   Nitric acid can be converted to nitrate compounds.

5.   Nitric acid is made in industry by the combination of nitrogen and oxygen.

6.   Nitrogen dioxide is produced in the air during lightning storms.

7.   Rain water containing dissolved nitrogen dioxide increases the pH of the soil.

8.   Nitric acid is used to make fertilisers.

9.   Nitric acid is made in industry by the oxidation of ammonia.

10.   Exhaust fumes from motor cars contain nitrogen dioxide.

General level

Questions 1 to 6 refer to the industrial manufacture of nitric acid.

Decide whether each of the following statements is

      A. TRUE   **B. FALSE.**

1.   The oxidation of ammonia is called the Haber Process.

2.   A platinum catalyst can be used in the reaction.

3.   In the presence of air, nitrogen dioxide dissolves in water to form nitric acid.

4.   The industrial manufacture of nitric acid is by the Ostwald Process.

5.   Hydrogen and oxides of nitrogen are the products of the reaction.

6.   The reaction which takes place on the catalyst is exothermic.

Questions 7 to 11 refer to the following experiment which is used to show the catalytic oxidation of ammonia in the lab.

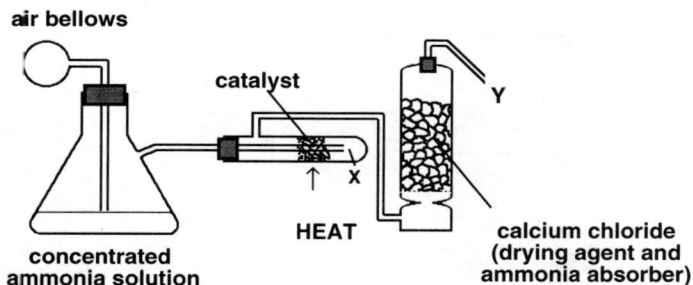

7.   What are the products of the reaction?

     A.   nitrogen and hydrogen

     B.   oxides of nitrogen and water

     C.   nitrogen and water vapour

     D.   oxides of nitrogen and hydrogen

8.   The main gaseous product coming out of **Y** is

     A. nitrogen dioxide   **B.** hydrogen

     C. ammonia   **D.** steam.

9. Pieces of pH paper can be placed at **X** and **Y**.

    These will show that the gases are

    A. acidic at **X** and alkaline at **Y**

    B. acidic at both **X** and **Y**

    C. alkaline at **X** and acidic at **Y**

    D. alkaline at both **X** and **Y**.

10. Which of the following catalysts is normally used for this reaction?

    A. iron

    B. vanadium pentoxide

    C. aluminium oxide

    D. platinum

11. Which graph would best show what happens to the mass of the catalyst as the reaction proceeds?

A.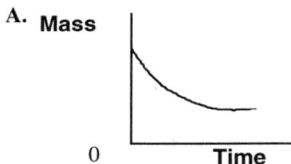

B.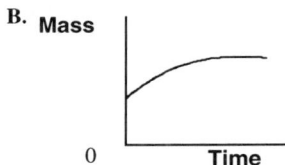

C.

D.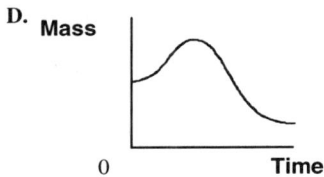

Credit level

Decide whether each of the following pairs of chemicals, when warmed,

    A. produces ammonia   **B.** does **NOT** produce ammonia.

1.   ammonium chloride / dilute nitric acid

2.   sodium nitrate / dilute sulphuric acid

3.   sodium hydroxide solution / ammonium sulphate

4.   dilute nitric acid / potassium hydroxide

5.   dilute hydrochloric acid / ammonium chloride

6.   sodium hydroxide / calcium nitrate

7.   potassium hydroxide solution / ammonium chloride

8.   ammonium carbonate / calcium hydroxide

9.   dilute sulphuric acid / ammonium chloride

10.   dilute nitric acid / calcium sulphate

Test 15.1   Respiration and photosynthesis

General level

In questions 1 to 15, decide whether each of the following statements is

     A. TRUE   **B.** FALSE.

1. Photosynthesis occurs in plants but **not** in animals.

2. Oxygen is used up during respiration.

3. Photosynthesis produces water vapour.

4. Carbon dioxide is required for respiration.

5. Respiration can occur in the dark.

6. Carbohydrates are made during photosynthesis.

7. Energy is released during photosynthesis.

8. Respiration occurs in both plants and animals.

9. Chlorophyll is required for respiration.

10. Photosynthesis can **not** occur in the dark.

11. Chlorophyll absorbs heat energy.

12. A gas produced during respiration will turn lime water milky.

13. Chlorophyll is used up during photosynthesis.

14. Respiration provides our bodies with energy.

15. Photosynthesis produces hydrogen gas.

Questions 16 to 18 refer to the following equations.

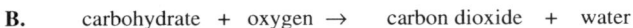

     A.   carbohydrate + water → carbon dioxide + oxygen

     B.   carbohydrate + oxygen →   carbon dioxide + water

     C.   carbon dioxide + oxygen →   carbohydrate + water

     D.   carbon dioxide + water →   carbohydrate + oxygen

16. Which equation represents photosynthesis?

17. Which equation represents respiration?

18. Which equation represents the combustion of a carbohydrate?

General level

In questions 1 to 6, decide whether each of the following elements is

    A. contained in a carbohydrate

    B. **NOT** contained in a carbohydrate.

1.	hydrogen	4.	carbon
2.	nitrogen	5.	oxygen
3.	sulphur	6.	iodine

Questions 7 to 10 refer to the products of the burning of carbohydrates.

Decide whether each of the following gases is

    A. produced in the reaction

    B. **NOT** produced in the reaction.

7.	hydrogen oxide	9.	carbon dioxide
8.	sulphur dioxide	10.	ammonia

In questions 11 to 18, decide whether each of the following substances

    A. can be classified as a carbohydrate

    B. can **NOT** be classified as a carbohydrate.

11.	sucrose	16.	$C_{12}H_{22}O_{11}$
12.	salt	17.	C_6H_{14}
13.	glucose	18.	$C_6H_{12}O_6$
14.	starch	19.	H_2O_2
15.	paraffin wax	20.	C_2H_6O

Test 15.3 Testing for carbohydrates

General level

Questions 1 to 7 refer to the following carbohydrates.

A. glucose **B.** starch

1. Which one has a sweet taste?
2. Which one dissolves well in water?
3. Which one when added to water reflects a beam of light?
4. Which shows a positive test with Benedict's Reagent?
5. Which shows a positive test with iodine solution?
6. Which produces a blue/black colour when the test is positive?
7. Which produces a brick red colour when the test is positive?

8. Sucrose can be positively identified using

A. Benedict's Reagent

B. iodine solution

C. neither.

9. A solution contained a mixture of two carbohydrates.

(i) It gave a blue/black colour with iodine solution.
(ii) It gave an orange precipitate when warmed with Benedict's Reagent.

The mixture could be

A. sucrose and glucose

B. starch and sucrose

C. starch and glucose.

General level

Decide whether each of the following statements is

A. TRUE   **B.** FALSE.

1. Glucose is built up during photosynthesis.

2. The joining up of glucose molecules to form starch is an example of a polymerisation reaction.

3. Starch is a polymer made in plants.

4. Starch is the carbohydrate which reacts with oxygen during respiration.

5. Glucose is the monomer used to build up starch.

6. Glucose breaks down to form starch during digestion.

7. Polymerisation of glucose takes place in plants.

8. Glucose molecules are small enough to pass through the gut wall.

9. Amylase plays a part in the digestion of starch.

10. Starch is produced during the digestion of glucose.

11. The breakdown of starch using saliva is best carried out at 70 $^{\circ}$C.

Credit level

Questions 1 and 2 refer to the tests using the following solutions.

    A. Benedict's Reagent   **B.** iodine solution

Which solution gives a positive test with each of the following.

1.   fructose

2.   maltose

In questions 3 and 4, decide whether each of the following statements is

    A. TRUE   **B.** FALSE.

3.   A substance which burns to produce carbon dioxide **must** be a hydrocarbon.

4.   A substance which burns to produce carbon dioxide **must** contain carbon.

Questions 5 and 6 refer to the following ratios of atoms of carbon, hydrogen and oxygen.

    A. $C_3H_6O_3$ **B.** $C_{12}H_{22}O_{11}$

    C. $C_6H_{12}O_6$ **C.** $C_{12}H_{24}O_{12}$

5.   What is the formula for a monosaccharide?

6.   What is the formula for a disaccharide?

Questions 7 to 11 refer to the following types of carbohydrate.

    A.   monosaccharide

    B.   disaccharide

    C.   polysaccharide

To which type does each of the following belong?

7.   starch

8.   glucose

9.   sucrose

10.   fructose

11.   maltose

12. The formulae, $C_6H_{12}O_6$ and $C_{12}H_{22}O_{11}$, represent two different different

    A. isomers   **B.** hydrocarbons

    C. isotopes   **D.** carbohydrates.

13. Glucose and fructose are isomers. This means that they

    A.   are both carbohydrates

    B.   are both monosaccharides

    C.   both have the same structure

    D.   both have the same molecular formula.

14. Which of the following is an isomer of sucrose?

    A. glucose   **B.** fructose   **C.** maltose   **D.** starch

Questions 15 to 17 refer to statements which can be applied to carbohydrates.

    A. It is an isomer of fructose.

    B. It is a disaccharide.

    C. It is a polymer.

    D. It can be hydrolysed to produce smaller molecules.

    E. It is formed from carbon dioxide and water during photosynthesis.

15. Which **two** statements can be applied to glucose?

16. Which **two** statements can be applied to maltose?

17. Which **two** statements can be applied to starch?

Questions 18 to 24 refer to reactions of glucose, sucrose and starch.

Decide whether each of the following statements is

    A. TRUE   **B.** FALSE.

18. Carbon dioxide is produced when glucose molecules join up to make starch.

19. The breakdown of sucrose is an example of hydrolysis.

20. Starch molecules break down by reacting with water molecules.

21. Glucose is produced from starch by a condensation reaction.

22. The breakdown of starch is an example of hydrolysis.

23. The reaction represented by the equation

    $2C_6H_{12}O_6 \quad \rightarrow \quad C_{12}H_{22}O_{11} \quad + \quad H_2O$

    is an example of hydrolysis.

24. Starch is made in plants from glucose by addition polymerisation.

General level

Decide whether each of the following statements is

    A. TRUE   **B.** FALSE.

1. Alcoholic drinks can be made from fruit or vegetables.

2. Oxygen gas is produced in the making of alcohol from carbohydrates.

3. Amylase is required for the making of alcohol.

4. Alcohol is produced from carbohydrates by an addition reaction.

5. A biological catalyst is called an enzyme.

6. Oxygen gas is used up in the making of alcohol from carbohydrates.

7. Distillation is a method of increasing the alcohol concentration in alcoholic drinks.

8. Alcohol is a poison.

9. Fermentation is a way of separating alcohol and water.

10. Ethanol is the name of the alcohol in alcoholic drinks.

11. An enzyme in yeast is required for fermentation.

12. More than one substance can be classified as an alcohol.

13. Carbon dioxide gas is produced in the making of alcohol from carbohydrates.

14. Glucose can be used to make alcohol.

15. Fermentation is a way of separating liquids due to a difference in boiling point.

16. Whisky (40% alcohol) is made by fermentation followed by distillation.

17. The manufacture of beer (5% alcohol) involves distillation.

18. At high concentrations, alcohol can destroy the enzyme responsible for fermentation of glucose.

19. An increase in temperature does not necessarily increase the speed of a reaction which is catalysed by an enzyme.

20. An increase in pH will always increase the speed of a reaction which is catalysed by an enzyme.

Symbols and formulae 1

Molecular representations

General level

In questions 1 to 10, write the chemical formula for each of the following substances.

1.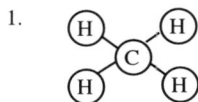

2.

3.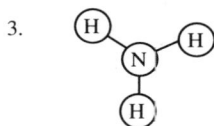

4.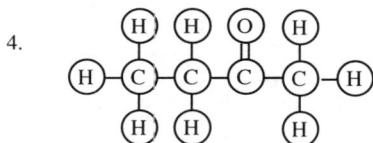

5.

6.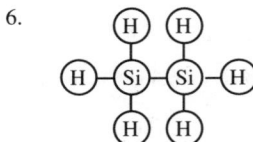

7.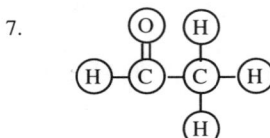

8.

9.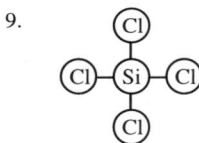

10.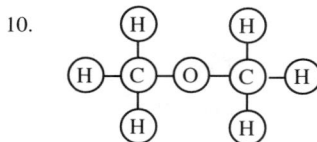

Assessment Tests for Standard Grade Chemistry

Questions 11 to 17 refer to the following arrangements of atoms.

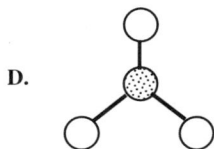

Which is a possible arrangement for each of the following substances?

11.   hydrogen oxide

12.   carbon tetrachloride

13.   hydrogen chloride

14.   oxygen

15.   phosphorus chloride

16.   nitrogen

17.   chlorine

Symbols and formulae 2

State symbols

General level

Write the state symbol for each of the following.

1. hydrogen gas

2. solid carbon

3. ethanol solution in water

4. liquid nitrogen

5. solid phosphorus

6. liquid sulphur

7. carbon dioxide solid

8. a solution of sulphur dioxide in water

9. bromine liquid

10. ammonia gas

Symbols and formulae 3 — Covalent compounds

General level

In questions 1 to 6, write the formula for the compounds formed from each of the following pairs of elements.

1. hydrogen and oxygen
2. hydrogen and chlorine
3. nitrogen and hydrogen
4. carbon and fluorine
5. phosphorus and chlorine
6. silicon and oxygen

In questions 7 to 12, write the formula for each of the following compounds.

7. nitrogen dioxide
8. carbon monoxide
9. sulphur trioxide
10. carbon tetrabromide
11. carbon dioxide
12. uranium hexafluoride

Symbols and formulae 4

Ionic compounds (i)

General level

Write the formula for each of the following compounds.

1. potassium chloride

2. magnesium bromide

3. calcium oxide

4. sodium sulphide

5. magnesium nitride

6. radium chloride

7. aluminium fluoride

8. aluminium oxide

9. sodium nitrate

10. lithium hydroxide

11. barium sulphate

12. potassium hydrogencarbonate

13. sodium phosphate

14. potassium hydroxide

15. calcium carbonate

16. ammonium chloride

17. lithium bromide

18. sodium carbonate

19. potassium sulphate

20. caesium fluoride

Symbols and formulae 5

Credit level

Write the formula for each of the following compounds.

1. copper(I) chloride

2. iron(II) oxide

3. iron(III) sulphide

4. copper(II) bromide

5. tin(IV) oxide

6. nickel(II) carbonate

7. calcium nitrate

8. aluminium sulphate

9. magnesium hydroxide

10. calcium hydrogensulphate

11. lead(II) nitrate

12. ammonium phosphate

13. aluminium nitrate

14. barium hydroxide

15. ammonium carbonate

Symbols and formulae 6   Mixed substances

General / Credit level

Write the symbol or chemical formula for each of the following substances.

1. lithium chloride

2. magnesium nitrate

3. nitrogen

4. potassium hydroxide

5. ammonium bromide

6. rubidium fluoride

7. magnesium sulphate

8. tin

9. sodium sulphide

10. carbon monoxide

11. hydrogen chloride

12. iron(III) chloride

13. calcium

14. bromine

15. strontium chloride

16. ammonium carbonate

17. iron(II) hydroxide

18. hydrogen iodide

19. sulphur trioxide

20. magnesium sulphide

Chemical equations 1

General level

Write word equations for each of the following reactions.

1. Petrol reacts with oxygen in a car engine to form carbon dioxide and water vapour.

2. In the body, glucose is formed when starch reacts with water.

3. Carbon monoxide burns with a blue flame to form carbon monoxide.

4. Plants make glucose from carbon dioxide and water vapour. Oxygen is released in this reaction.

5. Iron is made in the Blast furnace when iron oxide reacts with carbon monoxide. Carbon dioxide is also formed.

6. Ethene reacts with hydrogen to produce ethane.

7. Silver chloride can be prepared by the reaction of silver nitrate solution with sodium chloride solution. Sodium nitrate solution is also produced in the reaction.

8. Hydrogen peroxide solution decomposes to form water and a gas that relights a glowing splint.

9. When zinc is added to dilute hydrochloric acid, a solution of zinc chloride is formed, along with a gas that burns with a 'pop'.

10. The decomposition of copper carbonate produces copper oxide and a gas that turns lime water milky.

Chemical equations 2

General level

Write a sentence to describe each of the following reactions.

The first one is done for you.

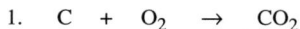

1. $C + O_2 \rightarrow CO_2$
   Carbon reacts with oxygen to form carbon dioxide.

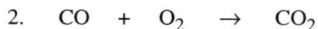

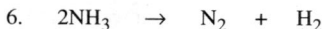

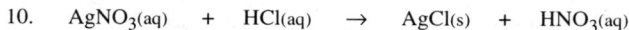

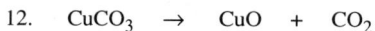

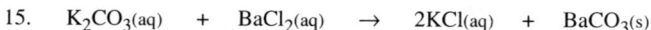

2. $CO + O_2 \rightarrow CO_2$

3. $H_2 + Cl_2 \rightarrow HCl$

4. $Si + Br_2 \rightarrow SiBr_4$

5. $SO_2 + O_2 \rightarrow SO_3$

6. $2NH_3 \rightarrow N_2 + H_2$

7. $Na + F_2 \rightarrow NaF$

8. $Fe + S \rightarrow FeS$

9. $CuO + H_2 \rightarrow Cu + H_2O$

10. $AgNO_3(aq) + HCl(aq) \rightarrow AgCl(s) + HNO_3(aq)$

11. $Mg + H_2SO_4 \rightarrow MgSO_4 + H_2$

12. $CuCO_3 \rightarrow CuO + CO_2$

13. $NH_4Cl + NaOH \rightarrow NaCl(aq) + H_2O(l) + NH_3(g)$

14. $3Mg + N_2 \rightarrow Mg_3N_2$

15. $K_2CO_3(aq) + BaCl_2(aq) \rightarrow 2KCl(aq) + BaCO_3(s)$

Chemical equations 3

General / Credit level

(a)   Use symbols and formulae to write chemical equations for each of the following reactions.

(b)   Balance the equations.

1.   carbon   +   oxygen $\rightarrow$ carbon monoxide

2.   sulphur dioxide   +   oxygen $\rightarrow$ sulphur trioxide

3.   hydrogen chloride $\rightarrow$ hydrogen   +   chlorine

4.   hydrogen   +   oxygen $\rightarrow$ hydrogen oxide

5.   phosphorus   +   chlorine $\rightarrow$ phosphorus chloride

6.   silicon   +   fluorine $\rightarrow$ silicon fluoride

7.   methane (CH_4)   +   oxygen $\rightarrow$ carbon dioxide   +   hydrogen oxide

8.   carbon   +   chlorine $\rightarrow$ carbon tetrachloride

9.   nitrogen   +   oxygen $\rightarrow$ nitrogen dioxide

10.   ammonia (NH_3)   +   oxygen $\rightarrow$ nitrogen   +   hydrogen oxide

11.   the burning of sulphur to form sulphur dioxide

12.   the reaction of silicon with chlorine

13.   the burning of ethene (C_2H_4) to form carbon dioxide and water

14.   the formation of hydrogen iodide

15.   the decomposition of nitrogen hydride

Chemical equations 4

General / Credit level

(a) Use symbols and formulae to write chemical equations for each of the following reactions.

(b) Balance the equations.

1. magnesium + oxygen → magnesium oxide

2. potassium + chlorine → postassium chloride

3. calcium + sulphuric acid → calcium sulphate + hydrogen

4. magnesium + sulphur dioxide → magnesium oxide + sulphur

5. barium chloride solution + sodium sulphate solution →
   sodium chloride solution + barium sulphate solid

6. calcium carbonate + hydrochloric acid →
   calcium chloride + carbon dioxide + water

7. lithium + hydrochloric acid → lithium chloride + hydrogen

8. sodium carbonate + nitric acid →
   sodium nitrate + carbon dioxide + water

9. potassium hydroxide + hydrochloric acid → potassium chloride + water

10. lithium oxide + nitric acid → lithium nitrate + water

11. sodium oxide + sulphuric acid → sodium sulphate + water

12. the burning of magnesium

13. the formation of potassium chloride from its elements

14. the reaction of aluminium with fluorine

15. the combination of sodium and bromine

16. the burning of aluminium

Chemical equations 5

Credit level

In questions 1 to 10, balance each of the following equations.

1. $C + O_2 \rightarrow CO_2$

2. $P + Cl_2 \rightarrow PCl_3$

3. $C + Br_2 \rightarrow CBr_4$

4. $C_4H_8 + O_2 \rightarrow CO_2 + H_2O$

5. $H_2O_2 \rightarrow H_2O + O_2$

6. $Mg + AgNO_3\text{(aq)} \rightarrow Mg(NO_3)_2\text{(aq)} + Ag$

7. $NaOH + H_2SO_4\text{(aq)} \rightarrow Na_2SO_4 + H_2O$

8. $AgNO_3\text{(aq)} + BaCl_2\text{(aq)} \rightarrow Ba(NO_3)_2\text{(aq)} + AgCl\text{(s)}$

9. $Na + H_2O \rightarrow NaOH + H_2$

10. $Al) + Cl_2 \rightarrow AlCl_3$

In questions 11 to 16, write balanced chemical equations for each of the following reactions.

11. iron + oxygen → iron(II) oxide

12. calcium + water → calcium hydroxide + hydrogen

13. magnesium hydroxide + nitric acid → magnesium nitrate + water

14. potassium sulphate solution + barium nitrate solution
→ potassium nitrate solution + barium sulphate solid

15. ammonia + dilute sulphuric acid → ammonium sulphate

16. lead(II) nitrate solution + potassium chloride solution
→ lead(II) chloride solid + potassium nitrate solution

Chemical equations 6

General / Credit level

(a) Write a word equation for each of the following reactions of acids.

(b) Use symbols and formulae to write equations.

(c) Balance the equations.

1. sodium hydroxide and nitric acid

2. calcium oxide and sulphuric acid

3. potassium carbonate and hydrochloric acid

4. magnesium and sulphuric acid

5. magnesium oxide and nitric acid

6. aluminium and sulphuric acid

7. iron(II) carbonate and hydrochloric acid

8. copper(II) hydroxide and nitric acid

(a) Write a word equation for each of the following precipitation reactions.

(b) Use symbols and formulae to write equations.

(c) Balance the equations.

(You may wish to refer to the Data Booklet.)

9. barium chloride solution and sodium sulphate solution

10. sodium carbonate solution and calcium chloride solution

11. silver nitrate solution ($AgNO_3$) and lithium chloride solution

12. lead chloride solution ($PbCl_2$) and sodium iodide solution

13. lead(II) nitrate solution and sodium chloride solution

14. sodium hydroxide solution and lead(II) nitrate solution

15. calcium nitrate solution and potassium carbonate solution

16. tin(II) chloride solution and barium hydroxide solution

Calculations 1   Relative formula mass

Credit level

Calculate the relative formula mass for each of the following substances.

1. CO_2

2. Mg_3N_2

3. C_2H_6

4. $CaSO_4$

5. Br_2

6. $Ca(NO_3)_2$

7. $Al(OH)_3$

8. C_3H_6O

9.   sulphur dioxide

10.   aluminium oxide

11.   hydrogen

12.   iron(III) hydroxide

13.   sodium carbonate

14.   ammonium carbonate

15.   carbon monoxide

16.   sodium phosphate

Calculations 2

The mole

Credit level

In questions 1 to 10, calculate the mass of one mole of each of the following substances.

1. NH_4NO_3

2. $Mg(OH)_2$

3. C

4. $(NH_4)_2SO_4$

5. C_2H_5OH

6. magnesium sulphate

7. silicon

8. copper(II) oxide

9. magnesium nitrate

10. calcium hydrogensulphate

In questions 11 to 20, calculate the mass of each of the following substances.

11. 2 mol of Cu

12. 0.1 mol of CO

13. 3 mol of CH_4

14. 1.5 mol of $Ca(OH)_2$

15. 10 mol of O_2

16. 2 mol of sodium sulphate

17. 0.5 mol of iron(II) hydrogensulphate

18. 1 mol of magnesium sulphide

19. 2.5 mol of potassium sulphate

20. 0.4 mol of helium

In questions 21 to 30, calculate the number of moles in each of the following substances.

21. 25 g $CaCO_3$

22. 72 g H_2S

23. 6.4 g S

24. 3.4 g NH_3

25. 8.4 g C_6H_{12}

26. 8.1 g magnesium oxide

27. 80 g sodium hydroxide

28. 1.6 g methane

29. 6.4 g copper(II) sulphate

30. 360 g glucose ($C_6H_{12}O_6$)

Calculations 3   Concentration

Credit level

1. How many moles of potassium hydroxide are required to make 200 cm^3 of solution, concentration 0.5 mol l^{-1} ?

2. What is the concentration of a solution of phosphoric acid, made by dissolving 0.5 mol of pure acid and making up to 250 cm^3 with water?

3. What volume of solution, concentration 2 mol l^{-1}, contains 0.1 mol of solute?

4. What is the concentration of a solution which contains 2 mol of hydrogen chloride dissolved and made up to 2 litres of solution.

5. How many moles of sodium hydroxide must be contained in 100 cm^3 of a solution, concentration 0.2 mol l^{-1} ?

6. What volume of a solution, concentration 0.2 mol l^{-1}, contains 0.05 mol of solute?

7. The formula mass of phosphoric acid is 98.

    If 49 g phosphoric acid is dissolved in water and the solution made up to 200 cm^3, what is the concentration of the resulting solution?

8. The formula mass of sulphuric acid is 98.

    What mass of pure sulphuric acid is required to make 100 cm^3 of solution, concentration 0.2 mol l^{-1}?

9. 52.5 g of pure citric acid (formula mass 210) is dissolved in water and the solution is made up to 500 cm^3.

    What is the concentration of the resulting solution?

10. What mass of pure sodium nitrate is needed to make 1 litre of solution, concentration 0.2 mol l^{-1}?

Calculations 4   Volumetric titrations

Credit level

1. What volume of hydrochloric acid, concentration $0.1 \text{mol } l^{-1}$ is required to neutralise 100 cm^3 of sodium hydroxide solution, concentration $0.1 \text{ mol } l^{-1}$?

2. What volume of sodium hydroxide solution, concentration $0.5 \text{ mol } l^{-1}$, will be neutralised by 50 cm^3 of sulphuric acid, concentration $0.2 \text{ mol } l^{-1}$?

3. If 100 cm^3 of nitric acid is neutralised by 50 cm^3 of potassium hydroxide solution, concentration $0.2 \text{ mol } l^{-1}$, what is the concentration of the acid?

4. What volume of sodium hydroxide solution, concentration $1 \text{ mol } l^{-1}$ will be neutralised by 50 cm^3 of hydrochloric acid, concentration $0.5 \text{ mol } l^{-1}$?

5. If 20 cm^3 of potassium hydroxide solution is neutralised by 50 cm^3 of sulphuric acid, concentration $0.1 \text{ mol } l^{-1}$, what is the concentration of the alkali?

6. What volume of hydrochloric acid, concentration $0.1 \text{ mol } l^{-1}$ is required to neutralise 10 cm^3 of potassium hydroxide solution, concentration $0.5 \text{ mol } l^{-1}$?

7. If 25 cm^3 of sodium hydroxide solution is neutralised by 14.4 cm^3 of nitric acid, concentration $0.22 \text{ mol } l^{-1}$, what is the concentration of the alkali?

8. What volume of sodium hydroxide solution, concentration $0.08 \text{ mol } l^{-1}$ will be neutralised by 17.6 cm^3 of sulphuric acid, concentration $0.1 \text{ mol } l^{-1}$?

9. What volume of nitric acid, concentration $0.12 \text{ mol } l^{-1}$ is required to neutralise 20 cm^3 of potassium hydroxide solution, concentration $0.1 \text{ mol } l^{-1}$?

10. If 20 cm^3 of sodium hydroxide solution is neutralised by 15.6 cm^3 of sulphuric acid, concentration $0.1 \text{ mol } l^{-1}$, what is the concentration of the acid?

Credit level

1. $CaCO_3 \rightarrow CaO + CO_2$

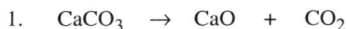

   What mass of carbon dioxide is produced by the decomposition of 10 g calcium carbonate?

2. $C_2H_4 + 3O_2 \rightarrow 2CO_2 + 2H_2O$

   What mass of water vapour is produced on burning 7 g of ethene?

3. $CuO + CO \rightarrow Cu + CO_2$

   What mass of copper oxide must be reduced to give 127 g of copper?

4. $2H_2 + O_2 \rightarrow 2H_2O$

   What mass of water vapour is produced on burning 1 g of hydrogen?

5. $2CO + O_2 \rightarrow 2CO_2$

   What mass of carbon monoxide must be burned to give 4.4 g of carbon dioxide?

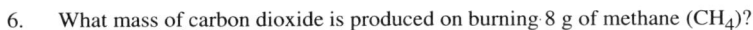

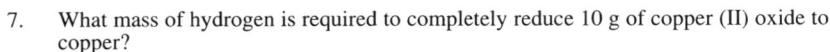

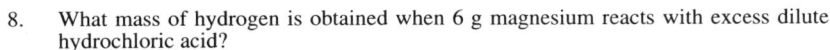

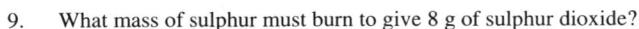

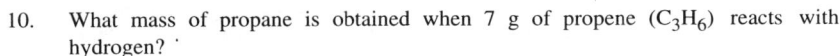

6. What mass of carbon dioxide is produced on burning 8 g of methane (CH_4)?

7. What mass of hydrogen is required to completely reduce 10 g of copper (II) oxide to copper?

8. What mass of hydrogen is obtained when 6 g magnesium reacts with excess dilute hydrochloric acid?

9. What mass of sulphur must burn to give 8 g of sulphur dioxide?

10. What mass of propane is obtained when 7 g of propene (C_3H_6) reacts with hydrogen?

Calculations 6   Simplest formulae

Credit level

In questions 1 to 3 calculate the simplest (empirical) formula for the following compounds from the percentage composition by mass.

1.   50% sulphur; 50% oxygen

2.   32% sodium; 23% sulphur; 45% oxygen

3.   15% magnesium; 19% nitrogen; 65% oxygen

4.   An analysis of an oxide of vanadium gave the following results.

     Mass of vanadium = 10 g;   Mass of oxygen = 8 g

     What is the formula for the oxide?

     (Take relative atomic mass of vanadium as 50.)

5.   Analysis of an oxide of antimony (Sb) gave the following results.

     Mass of antimony = 20 g ; Mass of oxygen = 4 g

     What is the formula for the oxide?

     (Take relative atomic mass of antimony as 120.)

6.   8 g of a hydrocarbon was shown on analysis to contain 6 g carbon.

     What is the formula for the hydrocarbon?

7.   56 g of an oxide of lead was strongly heated with carbon.

     When the oxide was completely reduced, 52 g lead remained.

     What is the formula for the oxide?

8.   A container when empty has a mass of 64 g. An oxide of copper was added and the mass of the container plus oxide was 82 g. Hydrogen gas was then passed over the heated oxide and after complete reduction the mass of the container plus copper metal was 80 g.

     What is the formula for the oxide?

Credit level

Calculate the percentage (by mass) of each of the elements present in the following compounds.

1. H_2O

2. CuO

3. NaOH

4. C_5H_{10}

5. $C_6H_{12}O_6$

6. copper(II) sulphate

7. calcium carbonate

8. silicon oxide

9. ammonium nitrate

10. magnesium sulphate

Chemical tests

General / Credit level

Questions 1 and 2 refer to the following colourless gases.

A.	hydrogen	**B.**	oxygen
C.	nitrogen	**D.**	carbon dioxide

1. Which gas relights a glowing splint?

2. Which gas burns with a 'pop'?

Questions 3 to 9 refer to the following solutions which are used in the laboratory for chemical tests.

A.	Benedict's Reagent	**B.**	bromine solution
C.	ferroxyl indicator	**D.**	iodine solution
E.	Universal indicator	**F.**	lime water

Which solution is used to test for each of the following?

3. an acid

4. carbon dioxide

5. the Fe^{2+} ions produced in rusting

6. an alkali

7. an unsaturated hydrocarbon

8. a sugar (but **not** sucrose)

9. starch

Question 10 to 16 refer to tests for gases.

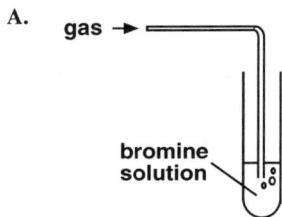

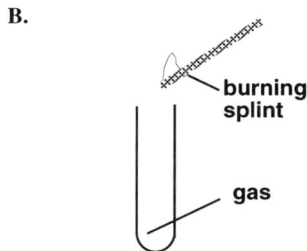

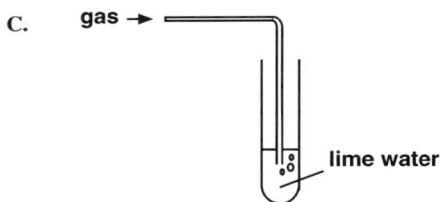

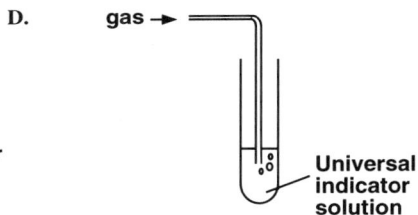

A.

gas →

bromine
solution

B.

burning
splint

gas

C.

gas →

lime water

D.

gas →

Universal
indicator
solution

Which test can be used to distinguish each of the following gases from nitrogen?

(Note that for some questions, more than one response may be correct.)

10.   oxygen

11.   carbon dioxide

12.   methane

13.   ammonia

14.   sulphur dioxide

15.   hydrogen

16.   ethene

17.   A solution contained a mixture of two carbohydrates.

It showed the following properties.
(i)   It gave a blue/black colour with iodine solution.
(ii)   It gave an orange precipitate when warmed with Benedict's reagent.

The mixture could be

A.   sucrose and fructose   **B.**   starch and sucrose

C.   starch and glucose   **D.**   glucose and fructose.

Types of reactions 1

General / Credit level

In questions 1 to 25, decide whether each of the following pairs of chemicals, **on heating if necessary**,

      A. react together   **B.** do **NOT** react together.

(You may wish to use the Data Booket.)

1.   potassium / water

2.   copper / dilute hydrochloric acid

3.   calcium oxide / sodium chloride

4.   ammonium sulphate / potassium hydroxide

5.   iron(II) chloride solution / sodium nitrate solution

6.   sodium carbonate / dilute sulphuric acid

7.   barium chloride solution / dilute sulphuric acid

8.   sodium hydroxide / dilute nitric acid

9.   magnesium sulphate / ammonium chloride

10.   lithium carbonate / sodium hydroxide solution

11.   iron / dilute sulphuric acid

12.   zinc / sodium chloride solution

13.   barium chloride solution / sodium carbonate solution

14.   magnesium carbonate / sodium sulphate solution

15.   copper(II) oxide / dilute nitric acid

16.   magnesium oxide / sodium hydroxide solution

17.   silver / copper(II) sulphate solution

18.   calcium / water

19.   silver nitrate solution / dilute hydrochloric acid

20.   magnesium / copper(II) sulphate solution

21.   calcium oxide / ammonium nitrate

22.   copper / water

23.   silver / dilute sulphuric acid

24.   iron(II) oxide / carbon monoxide

25.   potassium nitrate / magnesium carbonate

In questions 26 to 40, decide whether the reaction of each of the following pairs of chemicals

    A. produces a gas   **B.** does **NOT** produce a gas.

26.   ammonium chloride / sodium hydroxide solution

26.   calcium carbonate / dilute hydrochloric acid

28.   copper oxide / dilute sulphuric acid

29.   sodium hydroxide solution / dilute nitric acid

30.   sodium / water

31.   zinc / copper sulphate solution

32.   sodium chloride solution / silver nitrate solution

33.   magnesium / dilute sulphuric acid

34.   barium chloride solution / sodium sulphate solution

35.   ammonium sulphate / calcium hydroxide

36.   calcium / water

37.   zinc / dilute hydrochloric acid

38.   magnesium oxide / dilute nitric acid

39.   barium chloride solution / dilute sulphuric acid

40.   ammonium chloride / silver nitrate solution

Types of reactions 2

General / Credit level

The questions in this test refer to the following types of reaction.

A. addition	**B.** combustion	**C.** condensation	
D. cracking	**E.** displacement	**F.** fermentation	
G. hydrolysis	**H.** neutralisation	**I.** photosynthesis	
J. polymerisation	**K.** precipitation	**L.** redox	
M. respiration			

(Note that for some questions, more than one response may be correct.)

What type(s) of reaction can be applied to each of the following?

1. Energy is produced in the body from glucose.

2. Ethene reacts with bromine.

3. Zinc reacts with dilute hydrochloric acid.

4. Alcohol is produced from glucose.

5. Solid barium sulphate is produced by mixing barium chloride solution with sodium sulphate solution.

6. Starch is made from glucose in plants.

7. The molecules in oil fractions split up to form a mixture of saturated and unsaturated hydrocarbons.

8. Glucose is produced in plants from carbon dioxide and water.

9. Sodium hydroxide reacts with dilute hydrochloric acid.

10. Polythene is made from ethene.

11. Magnesium reacts with silver nitrate solution.

12. Dilute nitric acid reacts with sodium carbonate.

13. Magnesium combines with oxygen to form magnesium oxide.

14. Starch breaks down to form glucose.

15. $AgNO_3(aq)$ $+$ $NaCl(aq)$ $\rightarrow$ $AgCl(s)$ $+$ $NaNO_3(aq)$

16. $CH_3\text{-}CH=CH_2$ $+$ H_2 $\rightarrow$ $CH_3\text{-}CH_2\text{-}CH_3$

17. $C_6H_{12}O_6$ $+$ $6O_2$ $\rightarrow$ $6CO_2$ $+$ $6H_2O$

18. $Fe_2O_3(s)$ $+$ $3CO(g)$ $\rightarrow$ $2Fe(s)$ $+$ $3CO_2(g)$

19. $C_8H_{18} \rightarrow C_4H_8 + C_4H_{10}$

20. $Mg(s) + H_2SO_4(aq) \rightarrow MgSO_4(aq) + H_2(g)$

21. $KOH(aq) + HNO_3(aq) \rightarrow KNO_3(aq) + H_2O(l)$

22. $n\ CH_2{=}CH_2 \rightarrow (CH_2{-}CH_2)_n$

23. $Zn(s) + CuSO_4(aq) \rightarrow Cu(s) + ZnSO_4(aq)$

24. $n\ C_6H_{12}O_6 \rightarrow (C_6H_{10}O_5)_n + nH_2O$

25. $CH_2{=}CH_2 + Br_2 \rightarrow CH_2Br{-}CH_2Br$

26. $CuO(s) + H_2SO_4(aq) \rightarrow CuSO_4(aq) + H_2O(l)$

27. $C_6H_{12}O_6 \rightarrow 2C_2H_5OH + 2CO_2$

28. $2H_2O + 6CO_2 \rightarrow C_6H_{12}O_6 + CO_2$

29. $CaCO_3(s) + 2HNO_3(aq) \rightarrow Ca(NO_3)_2(aq) + CO_2(s) + H_2O(l)$

30. $CH_4 + 2O_2 \rightarrow CO_2 + 2H_2O$

31. $CH_2{=}CH_2 + H_2O \rightarrow CH_3{-}CH_2{-}OH$

32. $OH^-(aq) + H^+(aq) \rightarrow H_2O(l)$

33. $Ca^{2+}(aq) + 2F^-(aq) \rightarrow CaF_2(s)$

34. $2H^+(aq) + CO_3^{2-}(aq) \rightarrow H_2O(l) + CO_2(g)$

35. $Mg(s) + 2Ag^+(aq) \rightarrow Mg^{2+}(aq) + 2Ag(s)$

Problem Solving 1

Using the data booklet

General / Credit level

1. Which element was the first to be discovered?

   A. fluorine   **B.** lithium   **C.** magnesium   **D.** phosphorus

2. Which element has the highest density?

   A. copper   **B.** iron   **C.** silver   **D.** zinc

3. Which element has the highest melting point?

   A. chlorine   **B.** fluorine   **C.** nitrogen   **D.** oxygen

4. Which element has a boiling point of 280 $^{\circ}$C?

   A. aluminium   **B.** calcium   **C.** phosphorus   **D.** sodium

5. Which compound has a melting point of 712 $^{\circ}$C?

   A. barium chloride   **B.** lithium bromide

   C. magnesium chloride   **D.** potassium iodide

6. Which liquid has a boiling point of 69 $^{\circ}$C?

   A. pentane   **B.** hexane   **C.** heptane   **D.** octane

7. Which element has a red flame colour?

   A. barium   **B.** copper   **C.** lithium   **D.** sodium

8. A space probe sent to study the surface of the planet Mars would need to be made of a metal which would **not** melt at 510 $^{\circ}$C.

   Which metal could be used in this probe?

   A. magnesium   **B.** lead   **C.** tin   **D.** zinc

9. Metals used for making aircraft usually have a density of less than 3 g cm^{-3} and have to withstand temperatures up to 650 $^{\circ}$C.

    Which metal might be used for making aircraft?

Metal	Melting point/ $^{\circ}$C	Density/g cm^{-3}
A.	660	2.70
B.	98	0.97
C.	649	1.74
D.	1063	19.30

In questions 10 to 15, decide whether each of the following compounds is

    A. soluble in water   **B.** insoluble in water.

10. calcium carbonate

11. potassium chloride

12. iron(III) nitrate

13. barium sulphate

14. lead(II) iodide

15. sodium bromide

In questions 16 to 25, decide whether each of the following substances, **at the stated temperature**, is

    A. solid   **B.** liquid   **C.** gas

16. sodium at 100 $^{\circ}$C

17. copper at 1000 $^{\circ}$C

18. sulphur at 600 $^{\circ}$C

19. bromine at 0 $^{\circ}$C

20. nitrogen at –220 $^{\circ}$C

21. chlorine at 0 $^{\circ}$C

22. pentane at 50 $^{\circ}$C

23. barium chloride at 1000 $^{\circ}$C

24. sulphur dioxide at –5 $^{\circ}$C

25. magnesium chloride at 500 $^{\circ}$C

General / Credit level

Questions 1 to 3 refer to the following six experiments which were set up to investigate the dyeing of cloth.

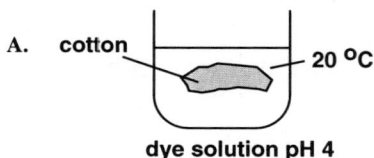

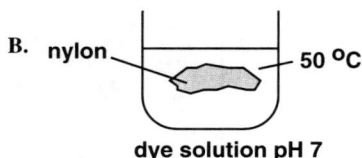

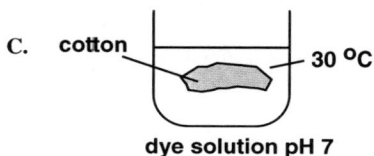

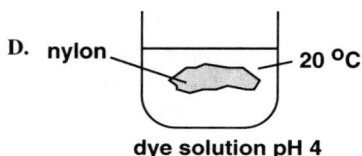

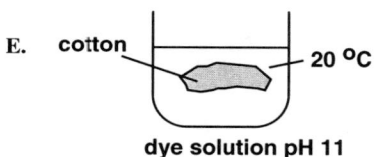

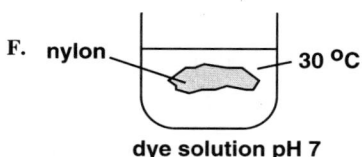

A.   cotton

20 °C

dye solution pH 4

B.   nylon

50 °C

dye solution pH 7

C.   cotton

30 °C

dye solution pH 7

D.   nylon

20 °C

dye solution pH 4

E.   cotton

20 °C

dye solution pH 11

F.   nylon

30 °C

dye solution pH 7

1.   Which **two** experiments should be compared to show the effect of pH on the dyeing of cloth?

2.   Which **two** experiments should be compared to show the effect of temperature on the dyeing cf cloth?

3.   Which **two** experiments should be compared to show the effect of dye on cotton and nylon?

Questions 4 to 6 refer to the following six experiments which were set up to study the reaction of magnesium with dilute hydrochloric acid.

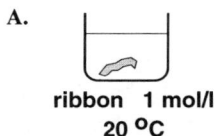

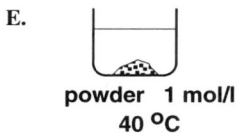

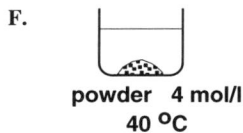

A.

ribbon   1 mol/l
20 °C

B.

powder 1 mol/l
20 °C

C.

ribbon   4 mol/l
20 °C

D.

ribbon   2 mol/l
30 °C

E.

powder 1 mol/l
40 °C

F.

powder 4 mol/l
40 °C

4.   Which **two** experiments could be used to show the effect of temperature on the rate of this reaction?

5.   Which **two** experiments could be used to show the effect of concentration on the rate of this reaction?

6.   Which **two** experiments could be used to show the effect of particle size on the rate of this reaction?

7.   A student carried out an experiment to find out whether Nightbrite or Daylite candles give out more heat when burned.

Which **two** arrangements could be used to make a fair comparison?

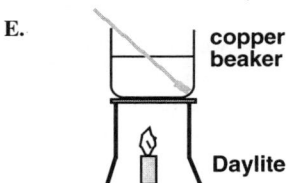

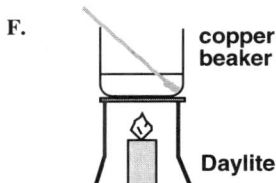

A.

aluminium
beaker

Nightbrite

B.

copper
beaker

Nightbrite

C.

aluminium
beaker

Nightbrite

D.

aluminium
beaker

Daylite

E.

copper
beaker

Daylite

F.

copper
beaker

Daylite

Questions 8 and 9 refer to the following six experiments which were set up to study the reactions of magnesium and iron with dilute hydrochloric acid.

A.

iron lump

1 mol/l   20 °C

B.

magnesium lump

2 mol/l   20 °C

C.

magnesium lump

2 mol/l   30 °C

D.

iron powder

1 mol/l   20 °C

E.

magnesium powder

2 mol/l   40 °C

F.

iron lump

2 mol/l   40 °C

8.   Which **two** experiments could be used to investigate the effect of temperature on the rate of reaction?

9.   Which **two** experiments could be used to investigate the effect of particle size on the rate of reaction?

10.   Some students set up the following experiments to study the sacrificial protection of metals. Each tube contains rust indicator.

Which **two** experiments would give a fair comparison of the ability of different metals to protect iron?

A.

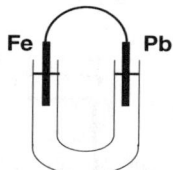

Fe   Pb

distilled water 30 °C

B.

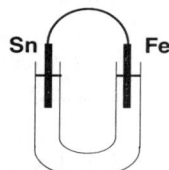

Sn   Fe

salt water 20 °C

C.

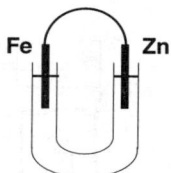

Fe   Zn

tap water 40 °C

D.

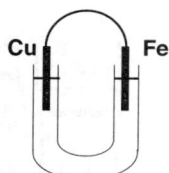

Cu   Fe

salt water 40 °C

E.

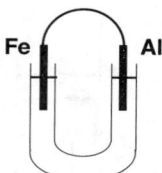

Fe   Al

tap water 20 °C

F.

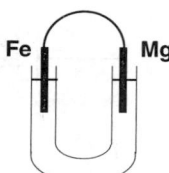

Fe   Mg

distilled water 30 °C

11. Hydrogen is produced by the electrolysis of sodium chloride solution. Six experiments were carried out.

	Concentration of solution (mol/l)	Type of electrode	Voltage (V)
A.	1.0	carbon	2.0
B.	2.0	platinum	4.0
C.	2.0	carbon	2.0
D.	2.0	platinum	2.0
E.	1.0	platinum	4.0
F.	4.0	carbon	4.0

Which **two** cells could be compared to investigate whether the voltage affects the volume of hydrogen produced?

Questions 12 and 13 refer to an investigation involving cells.

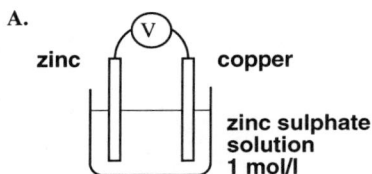

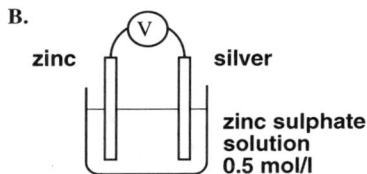

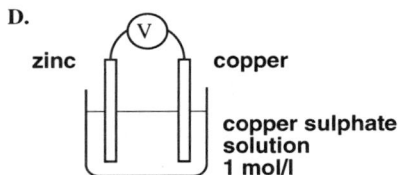

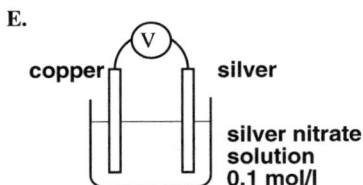

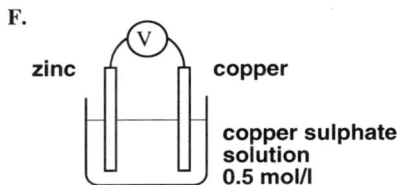

12. Which **two** cells could be compared to investigate whether the concentration of the electrolyte affects the cell voltage?

13. Which **two** cells could be compared to investigate whether the type of the electrolyte affects the cell voltage?

14. Jim was asked to find out whether fertilisers containing potassium ions, K^+, or fertilisers containing ammonium ions, NH_4^+, are better for growing lettuces.

He made up two fertilisers solutions for his experiment.

Which **two** solutions could Jim have used for a fair test?

A. KNO_3 concentration 1 mol/l   **B.** K_2SO_4 concentration 1 mol/l

C. K_2SO_4 concentration 2 mol/l   **D.** NH_4Cl concentration 1 mol/l

E. $(NH_4)_2SO_4$ concentration 1 mol/l   **F.** NH_4NO_3 concentration 2 mol/l

15. You have been asked to investigate whether vanadium or chromium is higher in the electrochemical series.

Which **two** cells could be compared to give this information?

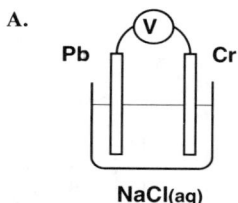

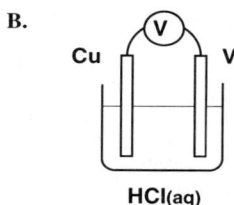

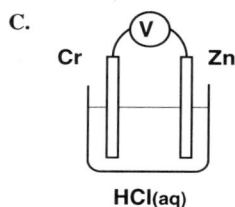

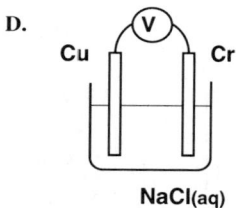

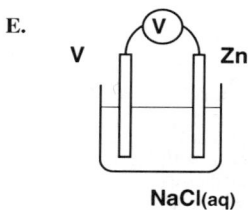

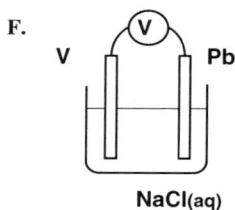

A. Pb | Cr — NaCl(aq)
B. Cu | V — HCl(aq)
C. Cr | Zn — HCl(aq)
D. Cu | Cr — NaCl(aq)
E. V | Zn — NaCl(aq)
F. V | Pb — NaCl(aq)

16.   Dissolved solids increase the boiling point of water.

Imran took some potassium nitrate solution and found the boiling point. He repeated his experiment using sodium nitrate solution.

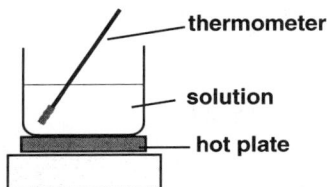

He then compared his results.

Which variable had to be the same for both experiments to make Imran's comparison fair?

A.   starting temperature of the solution   B.   temperature of the laboratory

C.   concentration of the solution   D.   size of the beaker

17.   John compared different brands of antifreeze.

He made a solution of each antifreeze and measured the freezing point.

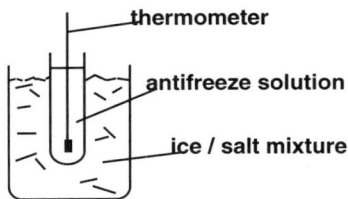

John wanted his comparison of freezing point to be fair.

Which variable had to be the same for all experiments?

A.   size of test tube   B.   concentration of solution

C.   volume of solution   D.   initial temperature of solution

18. A group of students carried out a project on shells – egg shells, snail shells and sea shells.

To compare the mass of calcium carbonate in the different shells, they added each shell sample separately to hydrochloric acid.

They used an **excess** of hydrochloric acid to make sure all the calcium carbonate in each sample had reacted.

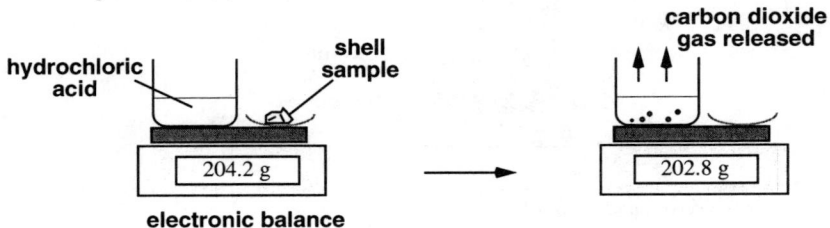

Which factor must be kept the same when comparing the mass of calcium carbonate in the different shells?

A. mass of shell samples   B. volume of acid

C. concentration of acid   D. particle size of shell samples

General / Credit level

1. Which apparatus would be most suitable for removing a soluble gas from a mixture of gases?

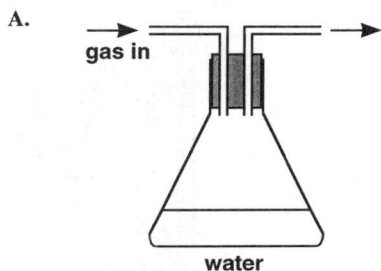

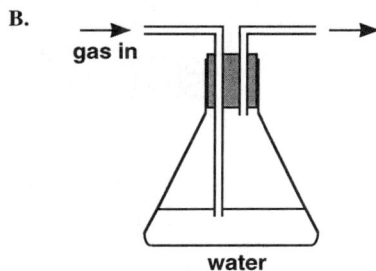

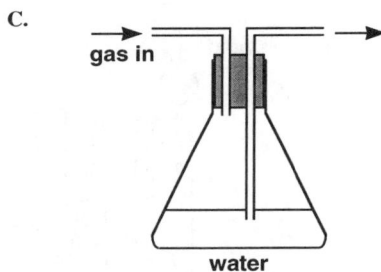

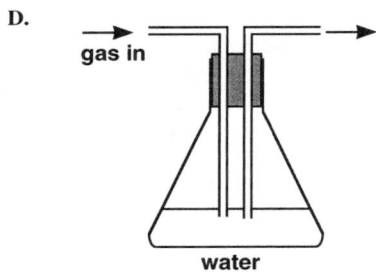

A.

gas in

water

B.

gas in

water

C.

gas in

water

D.

gas in

water

2. Nitrogen monoxide gas can be prepared in the laboratory by adding dilute nitric acid to copper turnings.

Nitrogen monoxide is insoluble in water and has a density similar to that of air.

Which arrangement is the most suitable for the preparation and collection of a sample of nitrogen monoxide?

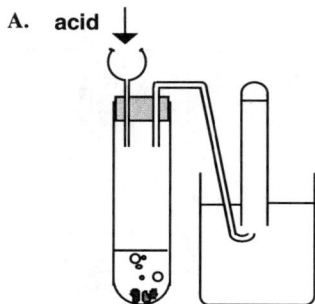

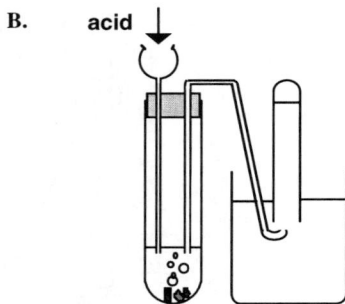

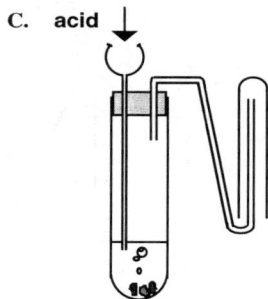

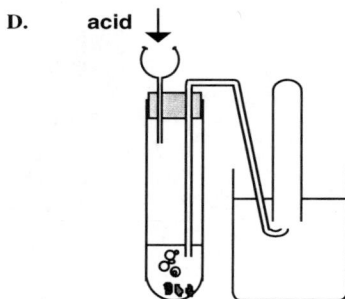

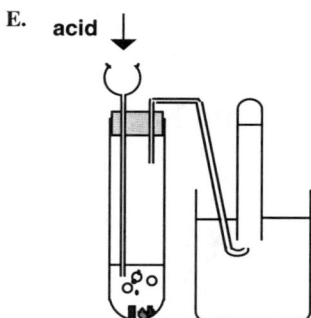

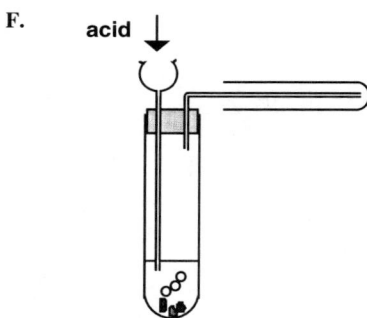

A. acid

B. acid

C. acid

D. acid

E. acid

F. acid

Questions 3 to 5 refer to methods of collecting gases.

A.

B.

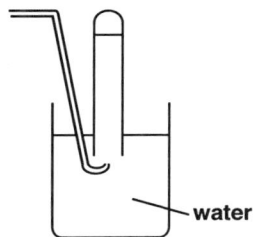

water

C.

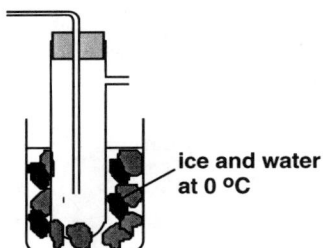

ice and water
at 0 °C

D.

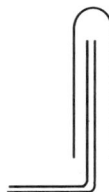

The following facts are known.

	Sulphur dioxide	Ammonia	Hydrogen
Solubility in water	Soluble	Soluble	Insoluble
Density compared to air	More dense	Less dense	Less dense
Boiling point	-10 °C	-33 °C	-253 °C

3. Which is the best method for collecting sulphur dioxide?

4. Which is the best method for collecting ammonia?

5. Which is the best method for collecting hydrogen?

6. When a sample of water is heated, any gases dissolved in the water are released as bubbles.

A student has to collect a sample containing **only** the gases dissolved in the water.

Which arrangement is the most suitable for collecting the sample of these gases?

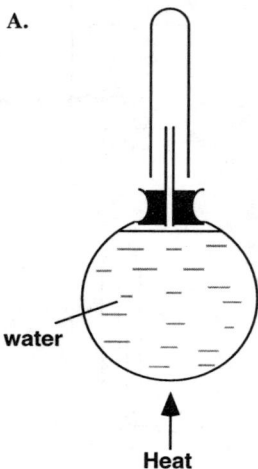

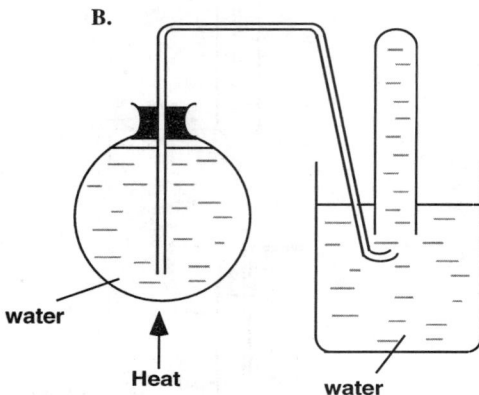

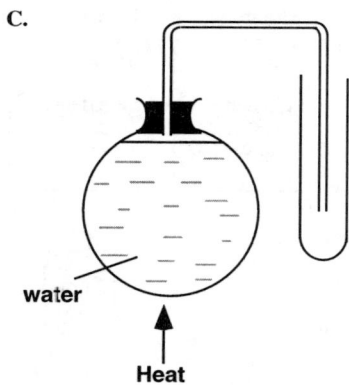

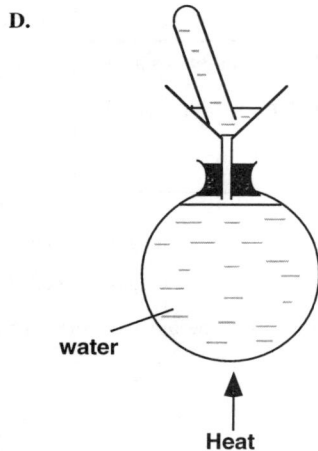

A.

water

Heat

B.

water

Heat

water

C.

water

Heat

D.

water

Heat

7. When gypsum is heated to produce plaster of Paris, water is driven off. This water can be collected.

Which apparatus would collect the water most efficiently?

A.

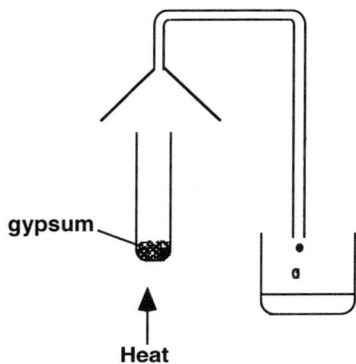

B.

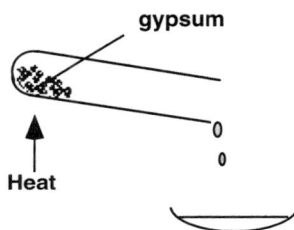

C.

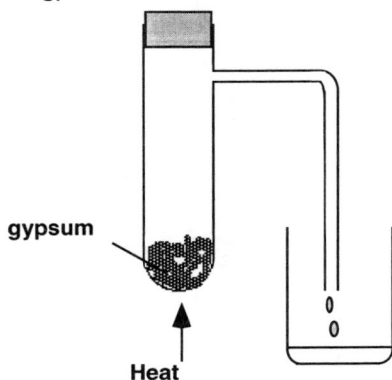

D.

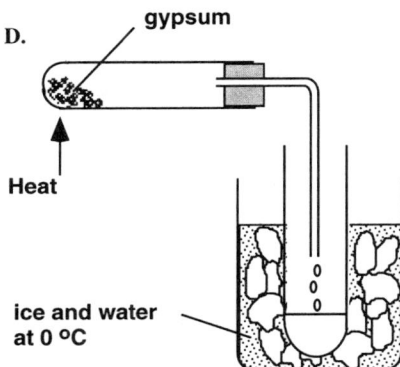

8. A student was asked to find the mass of copper in a sample of copper oxide.

   The student decided to change the oxide to copper metal, and measure the loss in mass.

   The apparatus, as it would appear half-way through the experiment, is shown.

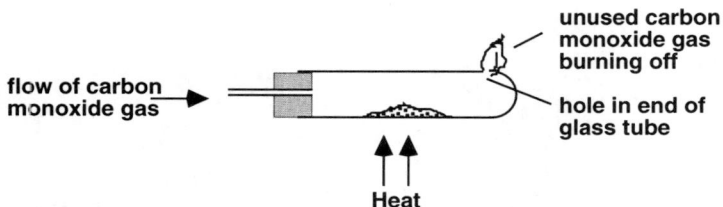

All of the following steps, **not** in the correct order, are used in the experiment.

A. Start the flow of carbon monoxide, light it at the hole, begin heating.

B. Weigh the glass tube and copper.

C. Weigh the glass tube and copper oxide.

D. Continue heating until all copper oxide has been changed to copper.

E. Stop heating, then 5 minutes later, stop the flow of carbon monoxide gas.

F. Weigh the glass tube empty.

Write down the letters for **all** the steps **in the correct order**.

9. A chemistry class carried out an experiment to find the mass of sodium chloride in a 100 g sample of a saturated solution.

All of the following steps, **not** in the correct order, are used in the experiment.

A.

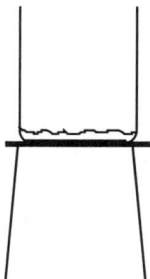

Allow to cool.

B.

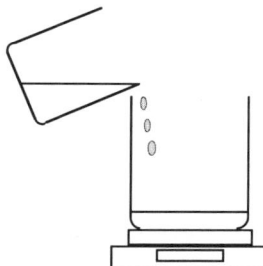

Take a 100 g sample of saturated solution.

C.

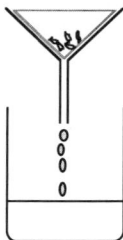

Filter the saturated solution.

D.

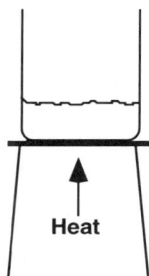

Heat

Boil dry.

E.

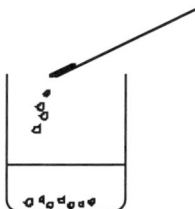

Make a saturated solution of sodium chloride.

F.

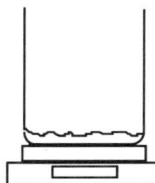

Weigh the sodium chloride left.

Write down the letters for **all** the steps **in the correct order**.

10. A student found the formula for magnesium oxide by the following experimental method.

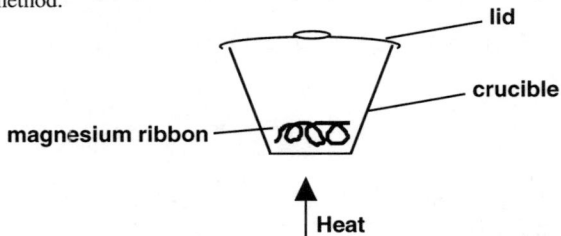

He made magnesium oxide by burning magnesium using the apparatus shown.

By measuring the change in mass, he was able to work out the masses of magnesium and oxygen in the sample of the compound.

All of the following steps, **not** in the correct order, are used in the experiment.

A. Weigh the crucible, lid and magnesium ribbon.

B. Clean the magnesium ribbon with emery paper.

C. Stop heating and allow crucible and contents to cool.

D. Weigh the crucible, lid and magnesium oxide.

E. Weigh the empty crucible and lid.

F. Heat the magnesium ribbon in the crucible.

Write down the letters for **all** the steps **in the correct order**.

11.

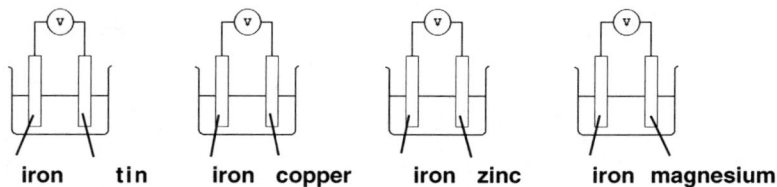

In order to place the metals in order of ability to supply electrons it is necessary to set up two more cells.

What two pairs are required?

A. tin/copper and magnesium/zinc

B. tin/magnesium and zinc/copper

C. tin/zinc and magnesium/copper

D. tin/zinc and zinc/copper.

12. Elizabeth was asked to find the approximate concentration of dissolved salts in a sample of sea water.

My plan

I will weigh a distillation flask and pour in some sea water. Then I will heat the sea water to dryness using the following apparatus

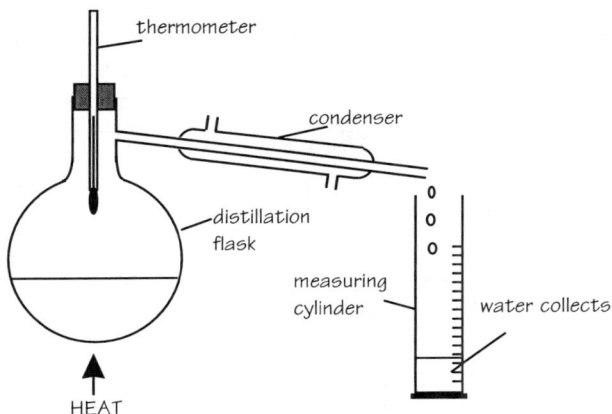

Which further measurement is needed by Elizabeth in order to calculate the approximate concentration of dissolved salts in sea water.

A.   boiling point of sea water

B.   volume of water which collects in the measuring cylinder

C.   time taken for the water to collect

D.   mass of empty measuring cylinder

E.   mass of distillation flask and remaining solid

Problem solving 4

General / Credit level

Questions 1 and 2 refer to the properties of five different elements.

Element **A.**	solid	metal	conducts electricity
Element **B.**	liquid	metal	conducts electricity
Element **C.**	solid	non-metal	does not conduct electricity
Element **D.**	solid	metal	conducts electricity
Element **E.**	solid	non-metal	conducts electricity

1. Which element could be carbon in the form of graphite?

2. The properties of which **two** elements do **not** support the view that only metallic solids conduct electricity?

Questions 3 to 9 refer to the burning of a solid compound in air.

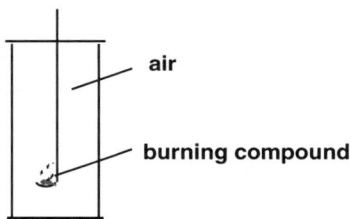

Large amounts of sulphur dioxide, and nitrogen were found in the mixture of gases present after burning.

For each of the following possible statements about the results, **on the evidence from the results alone**, decide whether the statement

A. **must** be true   **B.** **could** be true   **C.** can **NOT** be true.

3. The compound contained sulphur.

4. The compound contained oxygen.

5. The compound contained nitrogen.

6. The compound contained carbon and sulphur.

7. The compound contained carbon but not sulphur.

8. The compound contained sulphur but **not** nitrogen.

Questions 9 to 14 refer to an experiment in which Bill heated an unknown substance with copper oxide.

He found that **only** copper, water and carbon dioxide were formed.

For each of the following possible statements about the results, **on the evidence from the results alone**, decide whether the statement

    A.   **must** be true   **B.**   **could** be true   **C.**   can **NOT** be true.

9.   The substance contains carbon.

10.   The substance contains oxygen.

11.   The substance contains hydrogen.

12.   The substance contains copper, carbon and oxygen **only**.

13.   The substance is a carbohydrate.

14.   The substance is copper carbonate.

Questions 15 to 18 refer to the following experiment. It was carried out to estimate the percentage of oxygen in the air.

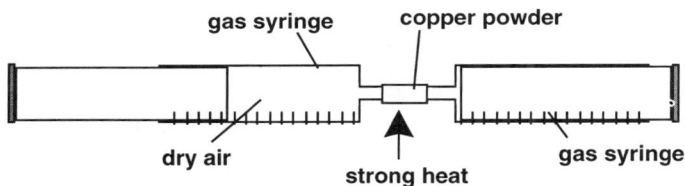

A 100 cm^3 sample of dry air was put into the left hand syringe. The copper was then heated and the air was passed back and forth from one syringe to the other. The hot copper reacts with the oxygen.

After some time, the heat was removed and the apparatus was allowed to cool.
The volume of gas left in the syringes was 85 cm^3.

Decide whether each of the following statements

    A.   could be used to explain this result

    B.   could **NOT** be used to explain this result.

15.   Heating was stopped too soon.

16.   The air was passed back and forward for too long.

17.   Not enough copper powder was taken.

18.   The air has more than the normal amount of oxygen.

Questions 19 to 24 refer to the following experiment. It was carried out to find the formula of a powdered substance in a bottle labelled 'copper oxide'.

The student reduced the copper oxide to copper metal, and measured the change in mass. This allowed the masses of copper and oxygen in the compound to be worked out.

The apparatus, as it would appear half-way through the experiment, is shown.

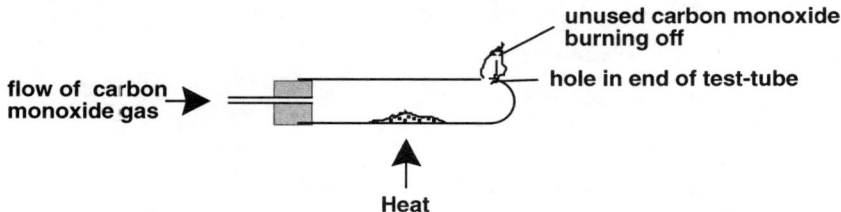

It was calculated that copper(I) oxide, Cu_2O, would lose 11% of its mass and copper(II) oxide, CuO, would lose 20% of its mass. The measured mass loss was 15%.

Decide whether each of the following statements

    A.   could be used to explain this result

    B.   could **NOT** be used to explain this result.

32.   The powder was copper(I) oxide; heating went on too long.

33.   The powder was copper(I) oxide; it was damp before it was heated.

34.   The powder was a mixture of copper(I) oxide and copper(II) oxide.

35.   The powder was copper(I) oxide; heating was stopped too soon.

36.   The powder was copper(II) oxide; carbon monoxide flow was stopped too soon.

37.   The powder was copper(II) oxide; the carbon monoxide flow was continued for too long.

Questions 1 to 4 refer to the characteristic flame colours of ions.

Different compounds were heated at the end of a rod and the resulting flame colours are shown in the table.

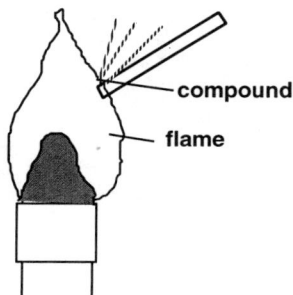

Compound	Flame colour
sodium chloride	yellow
copper(II) chloride	blue-green
potassium chloride	lilac
sodium sulphate	yellow
copper(II) sulphate	blue-green
potassium sulphate	lilac

Decide whether each of the following statements is

    A. TRUE   **B.** FALSE.

1. A compound containing copper(II) ions gives blue-green flames.

2. The lilac flame of potassium sulphate is due to the potassium ion.

3. Sulphate ions do **not** give a colour to the flames.

4. The yellow flame of sodium chloride is due to the chloride ion.

Questions 5 to 10 refer to a process called extraction.

Extraction means obtaining a pure metal from one of its compounds.

Decide whether each of the following equations

A.   represents the extraction of a metal

B.   does **NOT** represent the extraction of a metal.

5. $Zn_{(s)} + H_2O_{(g)} \rightarrow ZnO_{(s)} + H_2_{(g)}$

6. $SnO_2_{(s)} + C_{(s)} \rightarrow Sn_{(l)} + CO_2_{(g)}$

7. $CaCl_2_{(l)} \rightarrow Ca_{(s)} + Cl_2_{(g)}$

8. $Ni_{(s)} + 2HCl_{(aq)} \rightarrow NiCl_2_{(aq))} + H_2_{(g)}$

9. $2Ba_{(s)} + O_2_{(g)} \rightarrow 2BaO_{(s)}$

10. $FeO_{(s)} + CO_{(g)} \rightarrow Fe_{(s)} + CO_2_{(g)}$

Questions 11 to 16 refer to hard water, i.e. water which forms a scum when soap is added to it.

In an experiment to find out which ions make water hard, soap was added to various solutions. The results of the experiments are shown in the table.

Solution	Does a scum form?
sodium chloride	no
sodium nitrate	no
magnesium chloride	yes
sodium sulphate	no
iron(II) sulphate	yes
magnesium nitrate	yes

Decide whether each of the following ions

     A.   makes water hard   **B.**   does **NOT** make water hard.

11.   iron(II) ion   14.   chloride ion

12.   magnesium ion   15.   nitrate ion

13.   sodium ion   16.   sulphate ion

Questions 17 to 20 refer to the graph which shows how the solubilities of three salts vary with temperature.

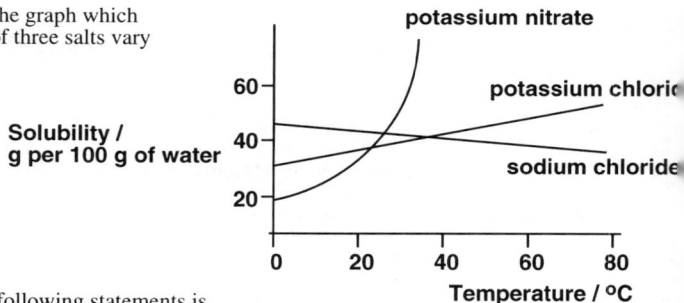

Decide whether each of the following statements is

     A.   TRUE   **B.**   FALSE.

17.   At 10 $^{\circ}$C potassium nitrate is more soluble than sodium chloride.

18.   At 20 $^{\circ}$C sodium chloride is more soluble than potassium chloride.

19.   At 40 $^{\circ}$C potassium chloride is more soluble than potassium nitrate.

20.   At 50 $^{\circ}$C sodium chloride is more soluble than potassium nitrate.

                                                 Assessment Tests for Standard Grade Chemistry

Questions 21 to 26 refer to alkanals and alkanones, two families of carbon compounds, each having the same general formula $C_nH_{2n}O$.

The two families differ because only the alkanals contain the following arrangement of atoms.

$$- \underset{\underset{O}{\|}}{C} - H$$

Decide whether each of the following structural formulae could represent

    A.   an alkanal

    B.   an alkanone

    C.   **neither** an alkanal **nor** an alkanone.

21.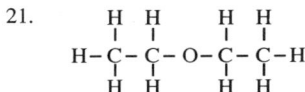

22.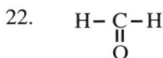

23.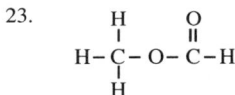

24.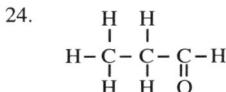

25.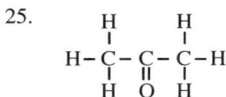

26.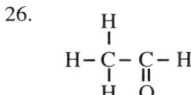

Questions 27 to 32 refer to compounds which contain hydrogen bonds.

Hydrogen bonds exist between molecules if the molecules contain a hydrogen atom directly bonded to a nitrogen **or** oxygen **or** fluorine atom.

Decide whether each of the following compounds

    A.   has hydrogen bonds between its molecules

    B.   does **NOT** have hydrogen bonds between its molecules.

27.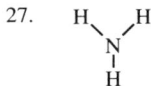

28.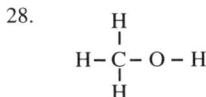

29.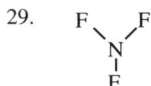

30. H – F

31.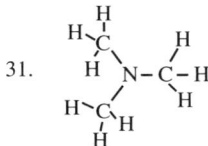

32.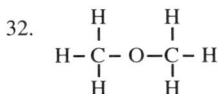

Questions 33 and 34 refer to alkanones and alkanoic acids, two families of carbon compounds.

Each family has a particular arrangement of atoms.

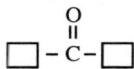   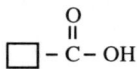

$$\begin{array}{cc} & O \\ & \| \\ \Box - C - \Box & \Box - C - OH \\ \text{alkanone} & \text{alkanoic acid} \end{array}$$

☐ represents the rest of the molecule

Alkanones can be prepared from alkanoic acids.

$$CH_3 - \overset{\displaystyle O}{\overset{\displaystyle \|}{C}} - OH \;+\; C_2H_5 - \overset{\displaystyle O}{\overset{\displaystyle \|}{C}} - OH \;\rightarrow\; CH_3 - \overset{\displaystyle O}{\overset{\displaystyle \|}{C}} - C_2H_5 \;+\; CO_2 \;+\; H_2O$$

The structural formulae for some alkanones are:

A.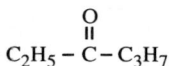

$$C_2H_5 - \overset{\displaystyle O}{\overset{\displaystyle \|}{C}} - C_3H_7$$

B.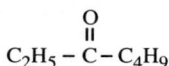

$$C_2H_5 - \overset{\displaystyle O}{\overset{\displaystyle \|}{C}} - C_4H_9$$

C.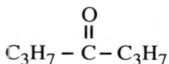

$$C_3H_7 - \overset{\displaystyle O}{\overset{\displaystyle \|}{C}} - C_3H_7$$

D.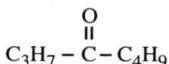

$$C_3H_7 - \overset{\displaystyle O}{\overset{\displaystyle \|}{C}} - C_4H_9$$

33.   Which alkanone can be produced from a mixture of the following alkanoic acids?

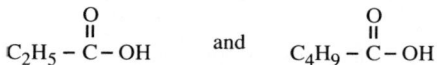

$$C_2H_5 - \overset{\displaystyle O}{\overset{\displaystyle \|}{C}} - OH \quad \text{and} \quad C_4H_9 - \overset{\displaystyle O}{\overset{\displaystyle \|}{C}} - OH$$

34.   Which alkanone can be prepared from only **one** alkanoic acid?

Questions 35 to 44 refer to hydration and dehydration reactions.

Hydration is the addition of the elements from water to a single compound; dehydration is the removal of the elements to make water from a single compound.

Decide whether each of the following reactions

    A.   is a hydration reaction

    B.   is a dehydration reaction

    C.   is **neither** a hydration **nor** a dehydration reaction.

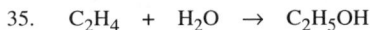

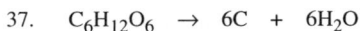

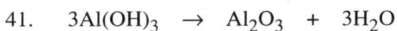

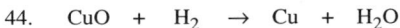

35. $C_2H_4 + H_2O \rightarrow C_2H_5OH$

36. $CH_4 + 2O_2 \rightarrow CO_2 + 2H_2O$

37. $C_6H_{12}O_6 \rightarrow 6C + 6H_2O$

38. $2H_2 + O_2 \rightarrow 2H_2O$

39. $C_2H_2 + H_2O \rightarrow C_2H_4O$

40. $HNO_3 + KOH \rightarrow KNO_3 + H_2O$

41. $3Al(OH)_3 \rightarrow Al_2O_3 + 3H_2O$

42. $Ca + 2H_2O \rightarrow Ca(OH)_2 + H_2$

43. $C_3H_7OH \rightarrow C_3H_6 + H_2O$

44. $CuO + H_2 \rightarrow Cu + H_2O$

General level

Questions 1 and 2 refer to the following hazard symbols.

A.    B.    C.

1.   Which hazard symbol would be found on a bottle containing petrol?

2.   Which hazard symbol would be found on a gas jar containing carbon monoxide?

Questions 3 and 4 refer to statements which can be applied to metals.

   A.   It conducts electricity.

   B.   It was discovered before 1800.

   C.   It is a solid at room temperature.

   D.   It is more reactive than potassium.

   E.   It is a transition metal.

   F.   It has a higher atomic number than silver.

(You may wish to use the Data Booklet.)

3.   Which **two** statements can be applied to **both** magnesium and mercury?

4.   Which **two** statements can be applied to copper but **not** to calcium?

Questions 5 to 12 refer to the following arrangements of atoms and molecules in pure substances and in mixtures.

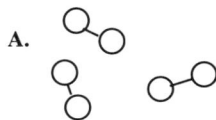

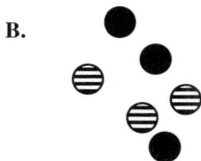

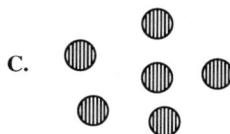

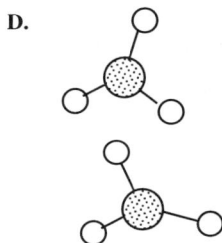

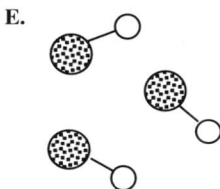

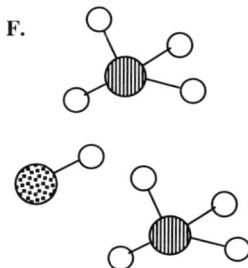

5. Which **two** arrangements can represent a pure element?

6. Which arrangement can represent a pure element made up of diatomic molecules?

7. Which arrangement can represent a mixture of elements?

8. Which **two** arrangements can represent a pure compound?

9. Which arrangement can represent a mixture of compounds?

10. Which arrangement can represent a pure compound made up of diatomic molecules?

11. Which arrangement can represent hydrogen fluoride?

12. Which arrangement can represent phosphorus hydride?

Questions 13 and 14 refer to statements which can be applied to hydrocarbons.

    A.   It is saturated.

    B.   It rapidly decolourises bromine water.

    C.   It contains three carbon atoms per molecule.

    D.   It contains a double bond between carbon atoms.

13.   Which statement can be applied to **both** ethane and propane.

14.   Which **two** statements can be applied to propene but **not** to propane.

Questions 15 to 19 refer to the pH of the substances shown in the diagram.

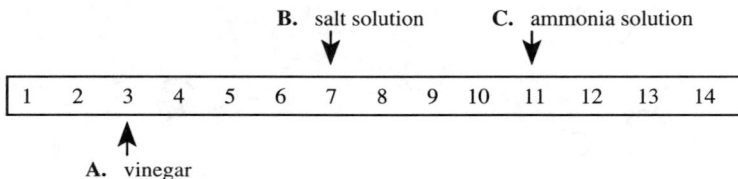

15.   Which solution is an acid?

16.   Which solution is an alkali?

17.   Which solution would show a decrease in pH when diluted with water?

18.   Which solution would show an increase in pH when diluted with water?

19.   Which solution would show no change in pH when diluted with water?

Questions 20 and 21 refer to statements which can be applied to acids.

    A.   It is neutral.

    B.   It has a pH of less than 7.

    C.   It forms compounds called nitrates.

    D.   It is a conductor of electricity.

    E.   It is the main acid in acid rain.

20.   Which **two** statements are correct about dilute hydrochloric acid?

21.   Which statement is true **only** for dilute nitric acid?

Questions 22 and 23 refer to coloured solutions made from fruits and flowers.

The colours of these solutions can be affected by pH.

		pH		
	Solution	Less than 7	7	Greater than 7
A.	hydrangea	pink	blue	yellow
B.	marigold	orange	orange	orange
C.	rose	pink	pink	yellow
D.	strawberry	red	red	green

22. Which solution gives a **different** colour with hydrochloric acid and with sodium chloride solution?

23. Which solution is **not** suitable for showing the difference between an acid and an alkali?

Questions 24 to 28 refer to a solution of citric acid, a solution which is found in oranges and lemons.

Decide whether each of the following statements is

    A. TRUE   B. FALSE.

24. The solution has a pH of more than 7.

25. The solution conducts electricity.

26. The solution reacts with copper metal.

27. The solution reacts with sodium carbonate.

28. The solution contains hydrogen ions.

Questions 29 and 30 refer to the addition of copper carbonate to dilute sulphuric acid.

The carbonate was added to the acid in a beaker until no more reacted.

The contents of the beaker were then filtered.

The solution in the flask was then evaporated to dryness.

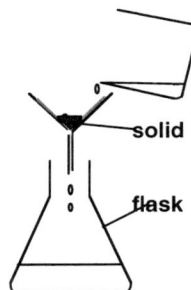

The names of some substances are:

A. copper oxide   B. copper carbonate

C. copper   D. copper sulphate

29. What was the name of the solid which collected in the filter paper?

30. What was the name of the solid which was left in the flask?

Problem solving   163

Questions 31 to 36 refer to the reaction of lumps of calcium carbonate with nitric acid.

Decide whether each of the following statements is

      A. TRUE   **B.** FALSE.

31.   The gas produced is hydrogen.

32.   The reaction produces calcium nitrate.

33.   The same gas will form if the acid used is hydrochloric.

34.   The same gas will form if the carbonate used is copper carbonate.

35.   The gas will be produced at the same rate if powdered calcium carbonate is used.

36.   The pH of the acid decreases as the reaction proceeds.

Questions 37 and 38 refer to experiments involving two different compounds, compound 1 and compound 2.

The results of the two experiments are shown below.

Compound	Flame test	Adding hydrochloric acid
1	Red	No change
2	Yellow	Gas given off which turns limewater milky

The names of some compounds are:

      A. copper sulphate   **B.** lithium sulphate

      C. sodium carbonate   **D.** sodium chloride

(You may wish to use the Data Booklet.)

37.   Which compound could have been compound 1?

38.   Which compound could have been compound 2?

Questions 39 and 40 refer to statements which can be applied to metals.

      A.   It reacts with dilute acid.

      B.   It reacts slowly with cold water.

      C.   It reacts when heated with oxygen.

      D.   It reacts with zinc sulphate solution.

      E.   It reacts with silver nitrate solution.

      F.   It reacts with sodium chloride solution.

39.   Which **two** statements can be applied to aluminium and copper?

40.   Which statement can be applied to magnesium but **not** to iron?

Questions 41 to 45 refer to a polymer called Alkathene.

Part of the structure of Alkathene is shown.

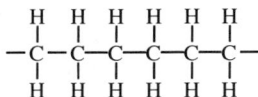

```
      H   H   H   H   H   H
      |   |   |   |   |   |
   —C — C—C—C—C—C—
      |   |   |   |   |   |
      H   H   H   H   H   H
```

Decide whether each of the following statements is

    A. TRUE   **B.** FALSE.

41.   It is biodegradable.

42.   It is a thermosetting polymer.

43.   It is produced when ethene is polymerised.

44.   It burns to produce carbon dioxide.

45.   It conducts electricity.

Problem solving 7

Credit level

Questions 1 to 6 refer to chemical reactions.

Decide whether each of the following reactions

      A. involves a catalyst   **B.** does **NOT** involve a catalyst.

1. the reaction of pollutants in car exhaust gases on the surface of platinum

2. the fermentation of glucose in the manufacture of beer

3. the burning of diesel in an engine

4. the digestion of starch to form glucose in the body

5. the sacrificial corrosion of magnesium attached to pipelines

6. the manufacture of ammonia from nitrogen and hydrogen by the Haber process

Questions 7 to 14 refer to the breakdown of hydrogen peroxide solution using a manganese dioxide catalyst.

$$2H_2O_2(aq) \quad \rightarrow \quad 2H_2O(l) \quad + \quad O_2(g)$$

hydrogen peroxide

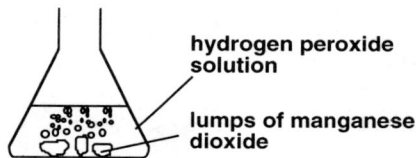

hydrogen peroxide solution

lumps of manganese dioxide

In questions 7 to 10, decide whether each of the following changes

      A. would increase the rate of the reaction

      B. would **NOT** increase the rate of the reaction.

7. heating the solution

8. powdering the manganese dioxide

9. increasing the volume of the solution

10. increasing the concentration of the solution

In questions 11 to 14, decide whether each of the following changes would

      A. increase the total mass of oxygen produced

      B. NOT increase the mass of oxygen produced.

11. heating the solution

12. powdering the manganese dioxide

13. increasing the volume of the solution

14. increasing the concentration of the solution

Question 15 to 19 refer to the information about the atoms shown in the table.

Atom	Atomic number	Mass number
P	22	50
Q	24	50
R	24	54
S	26	54
T	26	56

Decide whether each of the following statements is

    A. TRUE   **B.** FALSE.

15.   Atoms **P** and **Q** have the same number of protons.

16.   Atoms **Q** and **R** have the same number of electrons.

17.   Atoms **P** and **S** have the same number of neutrons.

18.   Atoms **R** and **S** are isotopes of each other.

19.   Atoms **S** and **T** have the same chemical properties.

Questions 20 to 24 refer to magnesium phosphide, a compound which is used in distress flares.

Decide whether each of the following statements is

    A. TRUE   **B.** FALSE.

20.   It has positive and negative ions in the ratio of two to three, respectively.

21.   It contains magnesium, phosphorus and oxygen.

22.   It conducts electricity if it is molten.

23.   It is made up of molecules.

24.   It is solid at room temperature.

Questions 25 and 26 refer to statements which can be applied to elements.

    A.   It is a non-metal.

    B.   It is in the same group as potassium.

    C.   It forms ions with a negative charge.

    D.   It is a solid at 25 °C.

    E.   It has the same number of occupied electron energy levels (shells) as calcium.

    F.   It has the same number of outer electrons as calcium.

25.   Which statement can be applied to **both** gallium and bromine?

26.   Which **two** statements can be applied to **both** strontium and barium?

Questions 27 to 32 refer to radium chloride.

Decide whether each of the following statements is

    A. TRUE   **B.** FALSE.

27.   The formula is $RaCl_2$.

28.   It is made up of molecules.

29.   It is insoluble in water.

30.   It conducts electricity in the solid state.

31.   The melting point is above 0 °C.

32.   It can be formed by the reaction of radium oxide with dilute hydrochloric acid.

Questions 33 to 39 refer to the following hydrocarbons.

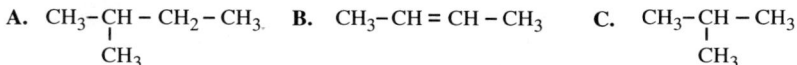

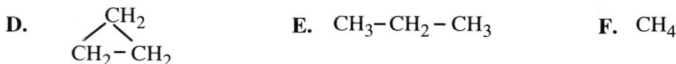

    A. $CH_3-CH-CH_2-CH_3$ **B.** $CH_3-CH=CH-CH_3$ **C.** $CH_3-CH-CH_3$

                 CH_3 CH_3

    D. CH_2 **E.** $CH_3-CH_2-CH_3$ **F.** CH_4

           CH_2-CH_2

33.   Which **two** hydrocarbons are **not** in the same homologous series as the hydrocarbon with molecular formula C_8H_{18}?

34.   Which hydrocarbon reacts with hydrogen to produce butane?

35.   Which hydrocarbon can form a polymer?

36.   Which hydrocarbon is an isomer of butane?

37.   Which hydrocarbon is an isomer of propene?

38.   Which hydrocarbon has the formula C_nH_{2n} but does **not** react with bromine solution?

39.   Which hydrocarbon has a relative formula mass of 58?

Questions 40 and 41 refer to statements which can be applied to hydrocarbons.

A.   It has isomers.

B.   It has the general formula C_nH_{2n}.

C.   It takes part in addition reactions.

D.   It contains only single carbon to carbon bonds.

E.   It does not react immediately with bromine water.

40.   Which **two** statements can be applied to **both** butene and cyclopropane?

41.   Which statement can be applied to butane but **not** to propane?

Questions 42 to 45 refer to the information about hydrocarbons which is shown in the table.

Hydrocarbon	Formula	Boiling point/°C	Flash point/°C
Hexene	C_6H_{12}	64	-9
Hexane	C_6H_{14}	68	-21
Cyclohexane	C_6H_{12}	81	-21
Heptane	C_7H_{16}	98	-4
Octane	C_8H_{18}	126	13

By referring to the data in the table, decide whether each of the following statements is

A.   TRUE   B.   FALSE.

42.   Octane will **not** flash at 0 °C.

43.   Isomers have the same flash point.

44.   The flash points of hydrocarbons increase as the boiling points increase.

45.   In a homologous series the flash point increases as the number of carbon atoms increases.

Questions 46 and 47 refer to statements which can be applied to solutions.

A.   It reacts with magnesium.

B.   It has a pH less than 7.

C.   It does **not** conduct electricity.

D.   It produces chlorine gas when electrolysed.

E.   The concentration of H^+(aq) ions in solution is equal to the concentration of OH^-(aq) in solution.

46.   Which **two** statements can be applied to **both** dilute hydrochloric acid and dilute sulphuric acid?

47.   Which statement can be applied to sodium chloride solution but **not** dilute hydrochloric acid?

Problem solving   169

Questions 48 to 53 refer to the addition of 20 cm³ of 1 mol/l sodium hydroxide solution to 20 cm³ of 1 mol/l sulphuric acid.

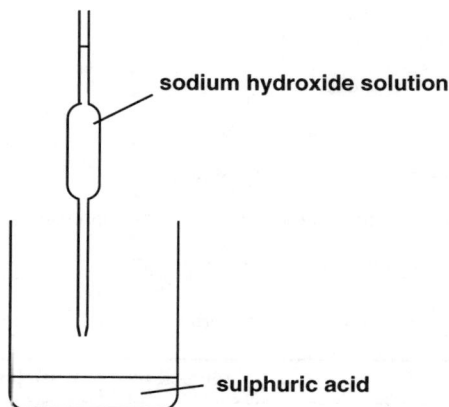

Decide whether each of the following statements is

    A. TRUE   **B.** FALSE.

48.   The number of $H^+_{(aq)}$ ions in the beaker increased.

49.   The pH of the solution in the beaker increased.

50.   The number of $SO_4^{2-}_{(aq)}$ ions in the beaker decreased.

51.   Water molecules formed during the reaction.

52.   The final solution contained equal numbers of $H^+_{(aq)}$ and $OH^-_{(aq)}$ ions.

53.   A precipitate was formed.

Questions 54 and 55 refer to statements which can be applied to acids.

    A.   Equal numbers of positive and negative ions are present.

    B.   A precipitate would be produced with barium hydroxide solution.

    C.   The $H^+_{(aq)}$ ion concentration would decrease when water was added.

    D.   Electrolysis would produce hydrogen gas at the negative electrode.

    E.   Two moles of sodium hydroxide would be neutralised by one mole of the acid.

54.   Which **two** statements can be applied to **both** dilute sulphuric acid and dilute hydrochloric acid?

55.   Which **two** statements can be applied to dilute sulphuric acid but **not** to dilute hydrochloric acid?

Questions 56 to 61 refer to the addition of water to hydrochloric acid, concentration 2 mol/l.

Decide whether each of the following statements is

    A. TRUE   **B.** FALSE.

56. The pH increases.

57. The acid is neutralised.

58. The concentrations of H^+(aq) ions increases.

59. The number of Cl^-(aq) ions in the solution decreases.

60. The volume of alkali needed for neutralisation decreases.

61. The speed of the reaction of the acid with zinc decreases.

Questions 62 to 66 refer to the pH values of 1 mol/l solutions of the salts which are shown in the table.

Salt	pH
Iron(III) sulphate	1
Aluminium chloride	3
Zinc sulphate	3
Copper(II) nitrate	3
Sodium chloride	7
Potassium sulphate	7
Sodium carbonate	10
Potassium carbonate	11

By referring to the data in the table, decide whether each of the following statements is

    A. TRUE   **B.** FALSE.

62. The salts are all neutral.

63. The salts of transition metals are all acidic.

64. The sulphate salts are all acidic.

65. The salts of Group 1 metals are all neutral.

66. The salts of hydrochloric acid are all neutral.

Questions 67 to 74 refer to hydrochloric acid, concentration 2 mol/l.

Decide whether each of the following statements is

A. TRUE   **B.** FALSE.

67.   When it is electrolysed, hydrogen is produced at the positive electrode.

68.   It contains more $H^+(aq)$ ions than $Cl^-(aq)$ ions.

69.   The speed of its reaction with iron is slower than with zinc.

70.   20 cm^3 is neutralised by 10 cm^3 of 2 mol/l sodium hydroxide.

71.   It is produced by dissolving one mole of hydrogen chloride in 500 cm^3 of water.

72.   It reacts with copper.

73.   It does not contain $OH^-(aq)$ ions.

74.   It reacts with calcium oxide to produce hydrogen.

Questions 75 to 81 refer to a flask which contains 2.0 litres of 0.10 mol/l sodium sulphate solution.

Decide whether each of the following statements is

A. TRUE   **B.** FALSE.

75.   No more than 0.10 mol of sodium sulphate is dissolved in the solution.

76.   Exactly 28.4 g of sodium sulphate was used to make it.

77.   It was made by dissolving the correct mass of sodium sulphate in exactly 2.0 litres of water.

78.   Sodium sulphate is the solute.

79.   Equal numbers of sodium ions and sulphate ions are present.

80.   More positively charged ions than negatively charged ions are present.

81.   It is a better conductor of electricity than pure water.

Assessment Tests for Standard Grade Chemistry

Questions 82 to 85 refer to the table which shows information about common gases.

Gas	Density of gas relative to hydrogen	Boiling point / °C
Methane	7	-182
Neon	9	-249
Carbon monoxide	12	-199
Oxygen	14	-218
Argon	18	-189

By referring to the data in the table, decide whether each of the following statements is

    A. TRUE   **B.** FALSE.

82.   Compounds have greater densities than elements.

83.   The density of a gas increases with the increase in relative formula mass.

84.   Gases which are diatomic elements have greater densities than monatomic elements.

85.   The boiling point of a liquid does not depend on the relative formula mass.

Questions 86 to 90 are about the volume of hydrogen produced from the reaction of metals with dilute hydrochloric acid.

Balanced equations can be used to calculate the volume of hydrogen produced.

Equation	Volume of hydrogen produced / litres
$Al(s)$ + $3HCl(aq)$ → $AlCl_3(aq)$ + $1\frac{1}{2}H_2(g)$	36
$Zn(s)$ + $2HCl(aq)$ → $ZnCl_2(aq)$ + $H_2(g)$	24
$Li(s)$ + $HCl(aq)$ → $LiCl(aq)$ + $\frac{1}{2}H_2(g)$	12

When each of the following reacts with dilute hydrochloric acid under the same conditions, decide whether the volume of hydrogen produced is

    A.   12 litres   **B.**   24 litres   **C.**   36 litres   **D.**   48 litres.

86.   14 g of lithium

87.   9 g of aluminium

88.   23 g of sodium

89.   60 g of calcium

90.   49 g of magnesium

Questions 91 and 92 refer to the following ion-electron equations.

A. $Fe(s) \rightarrow Fe^{2+}(aq) + 2e^-$

B. $Fe^{2+}(aq) + 2e^- \rightarrow Fe(s)$

C. $Fe^{2+}(aq) \rightarrow Fe^{3+}(aq) + e^-$

D. $Fe^{3-}(aq) + e^- \rightarrow Fe^{2+}(aq)$

E. $Cu(s) \rightarrow Cu^{2+}(aq) + 2e^-$

F. $Cu^{2+}(aq) + 2e^- \rightarrow Cu(s)$

91. Which equation shows iron(II) ions being oxidised?

92. Which **two** equations show the reactions which occur when an iron nail is placed in copper(II) sulphate solution?

Questions 93 and 94 refer to the redox reaction between iron(III) chloride solution and potassium iodide solution.

$$2FeCl_3(aq) + 2KI(aq) \rightarrow 2FeCl_2(aq) + I_2(aq) + 2KCl(aq)$$

The ions present during the reaction are:

A. $Fe^{3+}(aq)$ **B.** $Cl^-(aq)$

C. $K^+(aq)$ **D.** $I^-(aq)$

E. $Fe^{2+}(aq)$

93. Which ion is reduced?

(You may wish to use the Data Booklet.)

94. What are the **two** spectator ions in the reaction?

Questions 95 and 96 refer to statements which can be applied to reactions of metals.

A. It displaces lead from a solution of lead nitrate.

B. It reacts with cold water.

C. It can be obtained by heating its oxide with carbon.

D. It reacts with dilute hydrochloric acid.

E. It is displaced from a solution of its chloride by zinc.

95. Which **two** statements can be applied to **both** magnesium and tin?

96. Which statements can be applied to iron but **not** copper?

Questions 97 to 101 refer to experiments involving magnesium, zinc, copper, tin, silver and unknown metal **X**.

From all of their observations, a group of students produced the following order of reactivity.

silver, **X**, copper, tin, zinc, magnesium

⟶

Increasing reactivity

Decide whether each of the following observations

    A.   can be used to show that **X** has been wrongly placed

    B.   can **NOT** be used to show that **X** has been wrongly placed.

97.   Compounds of **X** were more readily reduced than compounds of zinc.

98.   **X** oxide was more stable to heat than silver oxide.

99.   **X** was more readily oxidised than copper.

100.   Magnesium displaced **X** from a solution of **X** nitrate.

101.   **X** reacted more vigorously with dilute acid than did tin.

Questions 102 to 106 refer to the voltages between pairs of metals.

Metal	Voltage / V	Direction of electron flow
P	0.6	metal → copper
Q	0.2	copper → metal
R	0.9	metal → copper
S	0.1	copper → metal

Decide whether each of the following statements is

    A. TRUE   **B.** FALSE.

102.   Metal **P** is the least reactive metal.

103.   Metal **R** is found uncombined in the Earth's crust.

104.   Metals **Q** and **S** are the easiest to obtain from their compounds.

105.   Metal **R** displaces the other metals from solutions of their salts.

106.   Metals **P** and **R** give a higher voltage than any other pair when connected in a cell.

Problem solving   175

Questions 107 to 112 refer to polyvinyl chloride, a plastic used to make pop records, clothing and pipes.

Decide whether each of the following statements is

A. TRUE   **B.** FALSE.

107.   (CH_2CHCl) is the repeating unit.

108.   It is an addition polymer.

109.   It is a thermosetting polymer.

110.   It is biodegradable.

111. $CH_2=CHCl$ is the monomer.

112.   It is a good conductor of electricity.

Questions 113 to 116 refer to the table which shows the solubilities of gases in water.

Gas	Volume of gas dissolving in 1 cm^3 of water at 20 °C
Ammonia	680
Carbon dioxide	0.848
Chlorine	2.26
Hydrogen	0.0182
Hydrogen chloride	442
Nitrogen	0.0152
Oxygen	0.030
Sulphur dioxide	39.4

By referring to the data in the table, decide whether each of the following statements is

A. TRUE   **B.** FALSE.

113.   The two most soluble gases both contain hydrogen.

114.   The acidic gases are more soluble than the alkaline gas.

115.   Chlorine is more soluble than the other gaseous elements.

116.   Chlorine is the most soluble of the diatomic molecules.

Questions 117 to 122 are about two branches of chemistry.

The study of chemicals which come from rocks, sea and air is called inorganic chemistry.

The study of chemicals which come from plants and animals is called organic chemistry.

Decide whether each of the following topics is most likely to be included

      A.   in an inorganic chemistry course

      B.   in an organic chemistry course.

117.   alcohol

118.   metals

119.   petrol and diesel

120.   plastics

121.   acids and alkalis

122.   sugars

Test 1.1	Test 1.2	Test 1.3	Test 2	Test 3.1	
1. A	1. A	1. copper chloride	1. A	1. A	19. C
2. A	2. A	2. sodium oxide	2. B	2. B	20. B
3. B	3. B	3. iron bromide	3. B	3. A	21. A
4. B	4. A	4. lead sulphide	4. A	4. B	22. B
5. B	5. A	5. hydrogen iodide	5. B	5. A	23. C
6. A	6. B	6. magnesium nitride	6. B	6. A	24. C
7. B	7. B	7. hydrogen and oxygen	7. A	7. B	25. A
8. B	8. A	8. copper, sulphur and	8. B	8. A	26. C
9. B	9. A	oxygen	9. A	9. A	27. B
10. A	10. B	9. magnesium and nitrogen	10. A	10. A	28. B
11. A	11. B	10. sodium, carbon and	11. B	11. B	29. C
12. B	12. A	oxygen	12. A	12. A	30. A
13. A	13. B	11. nitrogen and hydrogen	13. B	13. C	31. B
14. A	14. A	12. carbon and chlorine	14. A	14. A	32. B
15. B	15. B	13. sodium and sulphur	15. B	15. A	33. A
16. A	16. A	14. calcium, sulphur and	16. A	16. C	34. B
17. B	17. B	oxygen	17. B	17. A	35. A
18. A	18. B	15. potassium, nitrogen and	18. A	18. A	36. C
19. B	19. C	oxygen	19. S		
20. A	20. A	16. aluminium and bromine	20. Q		
21. B	21. B	17. sodium, phosphorus	21. R		
22. A	22. A	and oxygen	22. S		
23. A	23. C	18. potassium, chromium			
24. B	24. C	and oxygen			
25. B					

Test 3.2	Test 3.3	Test 3.4	Test 3.5	Test 3.6	Test 3.7
1. C	1. A	1. A	1. D	1. A	1. C
2. B	2. E	2. B	2. B	2. C	2. C
3. C	3. D	3. B	3. A	3. B	3. B
4. C	4. C	4. A	4. D	4. C	4. C
5. A	5. B	5. B	5. C	5. B	5. B
6. B	6. A	6. A	6. B	6. B	6. A
7. B	7. E	7. C	7. A	7. B	7. C
8. A	8. C	8. D	8. D	8. D	8. B
9. C	9. D	9. B	9. C	9. D	9. C
10. B	10. B	10. C	10. B	10. D	10. A
11. D	11. D	11. A	11. C	11. D	11. B
12. C	12. A	12. D	12. A	12. B	12. A
13. B	13. E	13. A	13. D		13. B
14. A	14. C	14. C	14. A		14. B
15. B	15. B	15. B	15. D		15. D
16. A	16. D	16. D	16. C		16. B
17. A	17. E	17. B	17. B		
18. B	18. D	18. D	18. B		
19. B	19. C	19. A	19. D		
20. A	20. D	20. C	20. A		
21. B			21. C		
22. A			22. D		
23. A			23. A		
24. B			24. C		
			25. B		

Test 3.8	Test 3.9	Test 4.1	Test 4.2	Test 5.1		Test 5.2
1. B	1. B	1. B	1. B	1. B	16. A	1. B
2. A	2. B	2. A	2. A	2. A	17. B	2. C
3. C	3. A	3. B	3. B	3. B	18. B	3. B
4. A	4. B	4. A	4. A	4. C	19. A	4. C
5. D	5. A	5. A	5. C	5. B	20. B	5. D
6. B	6. D	6. B	6. C	6. A	21. A	6. A
7. A	7. B	7. B	7. B	7. B	22. B	7. B
8. A	8. B	8. B		8. A	23. A	8. A
9. B		9. A		9. B	24. A	9. B
10. A		10. B		10. A	25. B	10. A
11. B		11. B		11. A	26. A	11. B
12. B		12. A		12. B	27. B	12. A
13. D		13. A		13. A	28. A	13. A
14. B		14. B		14. B	29. B	14. B
		15. B		15. A	30. B	15. A
		16. A				16. A
		17. A				17. A
		18. B				18. B
		19. A				19. A
		20. A				20. A
		21. B				21. B
		22. A				22. F
		23. B				23. D
		24. A				24. A
						25. E
						26. C

Test 5.3	Test 6.1	Test 6.2	Test 6.3	Test 6.4	Test 6.5
1. D	1. A, C	1. A	1. B	1. B	1. C
2. C	2. B, D	2. B	2. B	2. B	2. A, D
3. D	3. B, D	3. B	3. A	3. D	3. B
4. A	4. A, C	4. A	4. A	4. A	4. A, B, C
5. D	5. A, C	5. A	5. A	5. C	5. C, D
6. D	6. B, D	6. B	6. B	6. B	6. A, D
7. D	7. A, C	7. A	7. B	7. C	7. C, D
8. A	8. B, D	8. B	8. B	8. A	8. A, B
9. B	9. A, C	9. B	9. A	9. B	9. A, B, C
10. A	10. B, D	10. A	10. A	10. D	10. A, C, D
11. A	11. B, D	11. B	11. A	11. D	
12. A	12. A, C	12. A	12. B	12. D	
13. B	13. C	13. D, F, H	13. B	13. C	
14. A	14. G	14. D, F, H	14. B	14. D	
15. A	15. A	15. B	15. A	15. C	
16. B	16. D	16. B	16. A	16. D	
17. D	17. D	17. C	17. B	17. C	
	18. A	18. C	18. A	18. D	
	19. C		19. B	19. C	
	20. B		20. A	20. B	
	21. C		21. B		
	22. C		22. A		
			23. B		
			24. C		
			25. D		

Test 7.1

#	Ans	#	Ans
1.	A	17.	B
2.	B	18.	B
3.	A	19.	B
4.	A	20.	B
5.	B	21.	B
6.	B	22.	A
7.	A	23.	B
8.	A	24.	B
9.	B	25.	B
10.	A	26.	B
11.	B	27.	C
12.	B	28.	A
13.	A	29.	C
14.	B	30.	B
15.	A	31.	A
16.	A	32.	C
		33.	A

Test 7.2

#	Ans
1.	B
2.	A
3.	A
4.	B
5.	A
6.	A
7.	B
8.	B
9.	B
10.	B
11.	A
12.	B
13.	A

Test 7.3

#	Ans
1.	D
2.	A
3.	C
4.	A
5.	B
6.	C
7.	A
8.	D
9.	C

Test 7.4

#	Ans
1.	B
2.	A
3.	A
4.	B
5.	B
6.	A
7.	B
8.	A
9.	B
10.	B
11.	A
12.	C
13.	D
14.	C
15.	D
16.	A
17.	B
18.	D
19.	A
20.	B
21.	B
22.	A
23.	B
24.	D

Test 7.5

#	Ans	#	Ans
1.	A	26.	B
2.	C	27.	A
3.	B	28.	B
4.	B	29.	B
5.	A	30.	B
6.	C	31.	C
7.	B	32.	B
8.	A	33.	C
9.	A	34.	C
10.	B	35.	C
11.	A	36.	D
12.	B	37.	C
13.	B	38.	D
14.	A	39.	A
15.	B	40.	B
16.	A	41.	A
17.	B	42.	E
18.	A	43.	B
19.	B	44.	A
20.	A	45.	C
21.	B	46.	E
22.	A	47.	A
23.	B	48.	B
24.	A	49.	A
25.	A	50.	D

Test 8.1

#	Ans
1.	B
2.	C
3.	A
4.	A
5.	B
6.	C
7.	A
8.	B
9.	A
10.	A
11.	A
12.	A
13.	A
14.	B
15.	B
16.	A

Test 8.2

#	Ans
1.	B
2.	A
3.	A
4.	A
5.	B
6.	A
7.	B
8.	A
9.	B
10.	A
11.	B
12.	A

Test 8.3

#	Ans
1.	A
2.	B
3.	A
4.	C
5.	B
6.	B
7.	B
8.	C
9.	A
10.	C
11.	A
12.	B

Test 8.4

#	Ans
1.	A
2.	B
3.	B
4.	A
5.	A
6.	A
7.	B
8.	B
9.	B
10.	A
11.	B
12.	B
13.	B
14.	B

Test 9.1

#	Ans
1.	C
2.	B
3.	F
4.	B
5.	A
6.	C
7.	B
8.	A
9.	A
10.	B
11.	B
12.	A
13.	B
14.	B
15.	B
16.	A
17.	C
18.	A
19.	B
20.	A
21.	C
22.	A

Test 9.2

#	Ans
1.	B
2.	A
3.	A
4.	B
5.	B
6.	B
7.	A
8.	B
9.	A
10.	B

Test 9.3

#	Ans
1.	B
2.	A
3.	B
4.	B
5.	A
6.	A
7.	B
8.	A
9.	B
10.	B
11.	A
12.	B
13.	B
14.	A
15.	C
16.	A
17.	A
18.	C
19.	C
20.	B

Test 9.4		Test 10.1		Test 10.2		Test 10.4		Test 10.5		Test 11.1			
1.	A	1.	A	1.	A	1.	A	1.	A	1.	B	15.	A
2.	B	2.	A	2.	B	2.	B	2.	B	2.	D	16.	B
3.	A	3.	A	3.	A	3.	B	3.	A	3.	A	17.	B
4.	B	4.	B	4.	A	4.	B	4.	A	4.	C	18.	A
5.	A	5.	A	5.	B	5.	A	5.	B	5.	B	19.	D
6.	A	6.	A	6.	B	6.	B	6.	B	6.	A	20.	B
7.	A	7.	B	7.	B	7.	A	7.	B	7.	A	21.	C
8.	A	8.	B	8.	B	8.	A	8.	A	8.	A	22.	A
9.	B	9.	B	9.	A	9.	B	9.	B	9.	B	23.	B
10.	A	10.	A	10.	A	10.	A	10.	B	10.	B	24.	B
11.	B	11.	B			11.	A	11.	A	11.	A	25.	B
12.	A	12.	A			12.	B	12.	B	12.	B	26.	A
13.	B	13.	D	**Test 10.3**		13.	B	13.	A	13.	A	27.	A
14.	B	14.	C			14.	A	14.	B	14.	B	28.	B
15.	B	15.	C	1.	B	15.	B	15.	A				
16.	B	16.	C	2.	A	16.	A	16.	C				
17.	A	17.	A	3.	B	17.	A	17.	A				
18.	B	18.	A	4.	B	18.	A	18.	B				
19.	A	19.	B	5.	A			19.	A				
20.	B	20.	A	6.	B			20.	B				
		21.	B	7.	A			21.	B				
		22.	B	8.	A			22.	B				
		23.	A	9.	B			23.	A				
		24.	B	10.	A			24.	B				
		25.	A	11.	A								
				12.	B								

Test 11.2		Test 12.1		Test 12.2				Test 13.1		Test 13.2	
1.	B	1.	B	1.	A	17.	A	1.	B	1.	B
2.	A	2.	A	2.	A	18.	B	2.	A	2.	A
3.	B	3.	D	3.	B	19.	B	3.	B	3.	A
4.	A	4.	C	4.	A	20.	B	4.	A	4.	B
5.	B	5.	A	5.	B	21.	A	5.	A	5.	B
6.	B	6.	A	6.	A	22.	A	6.	A	6.	B
7.	A	7.	B	7.	B	23.	B	7.	B	7.	A
8.	A	8.	B	8.	B	24.	B	8.	B	8.	B
9.	B	9.	A	9.	C	25.	A	9.	A	9.	A
10.	A	10.	B	10.	B	26.	B	10.	A	10.	B
		11.	A	11.	B	27.	B	11.	B	11.	A
		12.	B	12.	B	28.	B	12.	B	12.	B
Test 11.3		13.	B	13.	A	29.	A	13.	B	13.	A
		14.	A	14.	A	30.	A	14.	A	14.	B
1.	A	15.	B	15.	B	31.	B	15.	A	15.	B
2.	A	16.	B	16.	B	32.	A	16.	A	16.	A
3.	D	17.	C					17.	B	17.	B
4.	C	18.	A					18.	A	18.	A
5.	D	19.	D					19.	A	19.	B
6.	B	20.	C					20.	B	20.	A
7.	B	21.	C					21.	B	21.	B
		22.	B					22.	A	22.	A
		23.	B								
		24.	B								
		25.	A								
		26.	D								
		27.	B								

Test 13.3	Test 14.1	Test 14.2	Test 14.3	Test 14.5	Test 15.1
1. A, B	1. A	1. B	1. B	1. B	1. A
2. A	2. A	2. B	2. B	2. A	2. A
3. A, C	3. B	3. A	3. B	3. A	3. B
4. A	4. B	4. A	4. A	4. A	4. B
5. B	5. A	5. A	5. A	5. B	5. A
6. B	6. B	6. A	6. A	6. A	6. A
7. C	7. A	7. B	7. A	7. B	7. B
8. B	8. B	8. B	8. A	8. A	8. A
9. C	9. A	9. B		9. C	9. B
10. A	10. A	10. A		10. D	10. A
11. D	11. B	11. B		11. C	11. B
	12. A	12. A			12. A
	13. A	13. B			13. B
	14. A	14. B			14. A
	15. A	15. A	**Test 14.4**	**Test 14.6**	15. B
	16. A	16. A			16. D
	17. A	17. A	1. B	1. B	17. B
	18. B	18. A	2. A	2. B	18. B
	19. A		3. A	3. A	
	20. A		4. A	4. B	
	21. B		5. B	5. B	
	22. A		6. A	6. B	
	23. A		7. B	7. A	
	24. A		8. A	8. A	
			9. A	9. B	
			10. A	10. B	

Test 15.2	Test 15.3	Test 15.5	Test 15.6	Symbols and formulae 1	Symbols and formulae 2
1. A	1. A	1. A	1. A	1. CH_4	1. (g)
2. B	2. A	2. A	2. B	2. Cl_2	2. (s)
3. B	3. B	3. B	3. B	3. NH_3	3. (aq)
4. A	4. A	4. A	4. B	4. C_4H_8O	4. (l)
5. A	5. B	5. C	5. A	5. HF	5. (s)
6. B	6. B	6. B	6. B	6. Si_2H_6	6. (l)
7. A	7. A	7. C	7. A	7. C_2H_2O	7. (s)
8. B	8. C	8. A	8. A	8. CS_2	8. (aq)
9. A	9. C	9. B	9. B	9. $SiCl_4$	9. (l)
10. B		10. A	10. A	10. C_2H_4O	10. (g)
11. A		11. B	11. A	11. E	
12. B		12. D	12. A	12. C	
13. A		13. D	13. A	13. A	
14. A		14. C	14. A	14. F	
15. B	**Test 15.4**	15. A, E	15. B	15. D	
16. A		16. B, D	16. A	16. B	
17. B	1. A	17. C, D	17. B	17. G	
18. A	2. A	18. B	18. A		
19. B	3. A	19. A	19. A		
20. B	4. B	20. A	20. B		
	5. A	21. B			
	6. B	22. A			
	7. A	23. B			
	8. A	24. B			
	9. A				
	10. B				
	11. B				

Symbols and formulae 3	Symbols and formulae 4		Symbols and formulae 5	Symbols and formulae 6	
1. H_2O	1. KCl	11. $BaSO_4$	1. CuCl	1. LiCl	11. HCl
2. HCl	2. $MgBr_2$	12. $KHCO_3$	2. FeO	2. $Mg(NO_3)_2$	12. $FeCl_3$
3. NH_3	3. CaO	13. Na_3PO_4	3. Fe_2S_3	3. N_2	13. Ca
4. CF_4	4. Na_2S	14. KOH	4. $CuBr_2$	4. KOH	14. Br_2
5. PCl_3	5. Mg_3N_2	15. $CaCO_3$	5. SnO_2	5. NH_4Br	15. $SrCl_2$
6. SiO_2	6. $RaCl_2$	16. NH_4Cl	6. $NiCO_3$	6. RbF	16. $(NH_4)_2CO_3$
7. NO_2	7. AlF_3	17. LiBr	7. $Ca(NO_3)_2$	7. $MgSO_4$	17. $Fe(OH)_2$
8. CO	8. Al_2O_3	18. Na_2CO_3	8. $Al_2(SO_4)_3$	8. Sn	18. HI
9. SO_3	9. $NaNO_3$	19. K_2SO_4	9. $Mg(OH)_2$	9. Na_2S	19. SO_3
10. CBr_4	10. LiOH	20. CsF	10. $Ca(HSO_4)_2$	10. CO	20. MgS
11. CO_2			11. $Pb(NO_3)_2$		
12. UF_6			12. $(NH_4)_3PO_4$		
			13. $Al(NO_3)_3$		
			14. $Ba(OH)_2$		
			15. $(NH_4)_2CO_3$		

Chemical equations 1

1. petrol + oxygen → carbon dioxide + water
2. starch + water → glucose
3. carbon monoxide + oxygen → carbon dioxide
4. carbon dioxide + water → glucose + oxygen
5. iron oxide + carbon monoxide → iron + carbon dioxide
6. ethene + hydrogen → ethane
7. silver nitrate solution + sodium chloride solution →
   silver chloride + sodium nitrate solution
8. hydrogen peroxide solution → water + oxygen
9. zinc + hydrochloric acid → zinc chloride + hydrogen
10. copper carbonate → copper oxide + carbon dioxide

Chemical equations 2

1. Carbon reacts with oxygen to form carbon dioxide.
2. Carbon monoxide reacts with oxygen to form carbon dioxide.
3. Hydrogen reacts with chlorine to form hydrogen chloride.
4. Silicon reacts with bromine to form silicon bromide.
5. Sulphur dioxide reacts with oxygen to form sulphur trioxide.
6. Ammonia decomposes to form nitrogen and hydrogen.
7. Sodium reacts with fluorine to form sodium fluoride.
8. Iron reacts with sulphur to form iron sulphide.
9. Copper oxide reacts with hydrogen to form copper and water.
10. Silver nitrate solution reacts with hydrochloric acid to form silver chloride and nitric acid.
11. Magnesium reacts with sulphuric acid to form magnesium sulphate and hydrogen .
12. Copper carbonate decomposes to form copper oxide and carbon dioxide .
13. Ammonium chloride reacts with sodium hydroxide to form sodium chloride, water and ammonia.
14. Magnesium reacts with nitrogen to form magnesium nitride .
15. Potassium carbonate solution reacts with barium chloride solution to form potassium chloride solution and barium carbonate solid.

Answers 183

Chemical equations 3

1. $2C + O_2 \rightarrow 2CO$
2. $2SO_2 + O_2 \rightarrow 2SO3$
3. $2HCl \rightarrow H_2 + Cl_2$
4. $2H_2 + O_2 \rightarrow 2H_2O$
5. $2P + 3Cl_2 \rightarrow 2PCl_3$
6. $Si + 2F_2 \rightarrow SiF_4$
7. $CH_4 + 2O_2 \rightarrow CO_2 + 2H_2O$
8. $C + 2Cl_2 \rightarrow CCl_4$
9. $N_2 + 2O_2 \rightarrow 2NO_2$
10. $4NH_3 + 3O_2 \rightarrow 2N_2 + 6H_2O$
11. $S + O_2 \rightarrow SO_2$
12. $Si + 2Cl_2 \rightarrow SiCl_4$
13. $C_2H_4 + 3O_2 \rightarrow 2CO_2 + 2H_2O$
14. $H_2 + I_2 \rightarrow 2HI$
15. $2NH_3 \rightarrow N_2 + 3H_2$

Chemical equations 4

1. $2Mg + O_2 \rightarrow 2MgO$
2. $2K + Cl_2 \rightarrow 2KCl$
3. $Ca + H_2SO_{4(aq)} \rightarrow CaSO_4 + H_2$
4. $2Mg + SO_2 \rightarrow 2MgO + S$
5. $BaCl_{2(aq)} + Na_2SO_{4(aq)} \rightarrow 2NaCl_{(aq)} + BaSO_{4(s)}$
6. $CaCO_3 + 2HCl_{(aq)} \rightarrow CaCl_2 + CO_2 + H_2O$
7. $2Li + 2HCl_{(aq)} \rightarrow 2LiCl + H_2$
8. $Na_2CO_3 + 2HNO_{3(aq)} \rightarrow 2NaNO_3 + CO_2 + H_2O$
9. $KOH + HCl_{(aq)} \rightarrow KCl + H_2O$
10. $Li_2O + 2HNO_{3(aq)} \rightarrow 2LiNO_3 + H_2O$
11. $Na_2O + H_2SO_{4(aq)} \rightarrow Na_2SO_4 + H_2O$
12. $2Mg + O_2 \rightarrow 2MgO$
13. $2K + Cl_2 \rightarrow 2KCl$
14. $2Al + 3F_2 \rightarrow 2AlF_3$
15. $2Na + Br_2 \rightarrow 2NaBr$
16. $4Al + 3O_2 \rightarrow 2Al_2O_3$

Chemical equations 5

1. $C + O_2 \rightarrow CO_2$
2. $2P + 3Cl_2 \rightarrow 2PCl_3$
3. $C + 2Br_2 \rightarrow CBr_4$
4. $C_4H_8 + 6O_2 \rightarrow 4CO_2 + 4H_2O$
5. $2H_2O_2 \rightarrow 2H_2O + O_2$
6. $Mg + 2AgNO_{3(aq)} \rightarrow Mg(NO_3)_{2(aq)} + 2Ag$
7. $2NaOH + H_2SO_{4(aq)} \rightarrow Na_2SO_{4(aq)} + 2H_2O$
8. $2AgNO_{3(aq)} + BaCl_{2(aq)} \rightarrow Ba(NO_3)_{2(aq)} + 2AgCl_{(s)}$
9. $2Na + 2H_2O \rightarrow 2NaOH + H_2$
10. $2Al + 3Cl_2 \rightarrow 2AlCl_3$
11. $2Fe + O_2 \rightarrow 2FeO$
12. $Ca + 2H_2O \rightarrow Ca(OH)_2 + H_2$
13. $Mg(OH)_2 + 2HNO_{3(aq)} \rightarrow Mg(NO_3)_2 + H_2O$
14. $K_2SO_{4(aq)} + Ba(NO_3)_{2(aq)} \rightarrow 2KNO_{3(aq)} + BaSO_{4(s)}$
15. $NH_3 + H_2SO_{4(aq)} \rightarrow (NH_4)_2SO_4$
16. $Pb(NO_3)_{2(aq)} + 2KCl_{(aq)} \rightarrow PbCl_{2(s)} + 2KNO_{3(aq)}$

Chemical equations 6

1. sodium hydroxide + nitric acid → sodium nitrate + water
   $NaOH + HNO_{3(aq)} → NaNO_3 + H_2O$

2. calcium oxide + sulphuric acid → calcium sulphate + water
   $CaO + H_2SO_{4(aq)} → CaSO_4 + H_2O$

3. potassium carbonate + hydrochloric acid → potassium chloride + carbon dioxide + water
   $K_2CO_3 + 2HCl_{(aq)} → 2KCl + CO_2 + H_2O$

4. magnesium + sulphuric acid → magnesium sulphate + hydrogen
   $Mg + H_2SO_{4(aq)} → MgSO_4 + H_2$

5. magnesium oxide + nitric acid → magnesium nitrate + water
   $MgO + 2HNO_{3(aq)} → Mg(NO_3)_2 + H_2O$

6. aluminium + sulphuric acid → aluminium sulphate + hydrogen
   $2Al + 3H_2SO_{4(aq)} → Al_2(SO_4)_3 + 3H_2$

7. iron(II) carbonate + hydrochloric acid → iron(II) chloride + carbon dioxide + water
   $FeCO_3 + 2HCl_{(aq)} → FeCl_2 + CO_2 + H_2O$

8. copper(II) hydroxide + nitric acid → copper(II) nitrate + water
   $Cu(OH)_2 + 2HNO_{3(aq)} → Cu(NO_3)_2 + 2H_2O$

9. barium chloride solution + sodium sulphate solution →
   sodium chloride solution + barium sulphate
   $BaCl_{2(aq)} + Na_2SO_{4(aq)} → 2NaCl_{(aq)} + BaSO_{4(s)}$

10. sodium carbonate solution + calcium chloride solution →
    sodium chloridesolution + calcium carbonate
    $Na_2CO_{3(aq)} + CaCl_{2(aq)} → 2NaCl_{(aq)} + CaCO_{3(s)}$

11. silver nitrate solution + lithium chloride solution → lithium nitrate solution + silver chloride
    $AgNO_{3(aq)} + LiCl_{(aq)} → LiNO_{3(aq)} + AgCl_{(s)}$

12. lead chloride solution + sodium iodide solution → sodium chloride solution + lead iodide
    $PbCl_{2(aq)} + 2NaI_{(aq)} → 2NaCl_{(aq)} + PbI_{2(s)}$

13. lead(II) nitrate solution + sodium chloride solution → sodium nitrate solution + lead(II) chloride
    $Pb(NO_3)_{2(aq)} + 2NaCl_{(aq)} → 2NaNO_{3(aq)} + PbCl_{2(s)}$

14. sodium hydroxide solution + lead(II) nitrate solution →
    sodium nitrate solution + lead(II) hydroxide
    $2NaOH_{(aq)} + Pb(NO_3)_{2(aq)} → 2NaNO_{3(aq)} + Pb(OH)_{2(s)}$

15. calcium nitrate solution + potassium carbonate solution →
    potassium nitrate solution + calcium carbonate
    $Ca(NO_3)_{2(aq)} + K_2CO_{3(aq)} → 2KNO_{3(aq)} + CaCO_{3(s)}$

16. tin(II) chloride solution + barium hydroxide solution →
    barium chloride solution + tin(II)hydroxide
    $SnCl_{2(aq)} + Ba(OH)_{2(aq)} → BaCl_{2(aq)} + Sn(OH)_{2(s)}$

Answers 185

Calculations 1

1. 44
2. 101.5
3. 30
4. 136
5. 160
6. 164
7. 78
8. 58
9. 64
10. 102
11. 2
12. 107
13. 106
14. 78
15. 28
16. 164

Calculations 2

1. 80 g
2. 58.5 g
3. 12 g
4. 132 g
5. 46 g
6. 120.5 g
7. 28 g
8. 79.5 g
9. 148.5 g
10. 234 g
11. 127 g
12. 2.8 g
13. 48 g
14. 101 g
15. 320 g
16. 284 g
17. 125 g
18. 56.5 g
19. 435 g
20. 1.6 g
21. 0.25
22. 2.1
23. 0.2
24. 0.2
25. 0.1
26. 0.2
27. 2
28. 0.1
29. 0.04
30. 2

Calculations 3

1. 0.1
2. 2 mol l^{-1}
3. 50 cm^3
4. 1 mol l^{-1}
5. 0.02
6. 250 cm^3
7. 2.5 mol l^{-1}
8. 1.96 g
9. 0.5 mol l^{-1}
10. 17 g

Calculations 4

1. 100 cm^3
2. 40 cm^3
3. 0.1 mol l^{-1}
4. 25 cm^3
5. 0.5 mol l^{-1}
6. 50 cm^3
7. 0.13 mol l^{-1}
8. 44 cm^3
9. 16.7 cm^3
10. 0.156 mol l^{-1}

Calculations 5

1. 4.4 g
2. 9 g
3. 159 g
4. 9 g
5. 2.8 g
6. 22 g
7. 0.25 g
8. 0.49 g
9. 4 g
10. 7.3 g

Calculations 6

1. SO_2
2. Na_2SO_4
3. MgN_2O_6
4. V_2O_5
5. Sb_2O_3
6. CH_4
7. PbO
8. Cu_2O

Calculations 7

1. hydrogen 11.1%, oxygen 88.9 %
2. copper 79.9%, oxygen 20.1%
3. sodium 57.5%, oxygen 40%, hydrogen 2.5%
4. carbon 85.7%, hydrogen 14.3%
5. carbon 40%, hydrogen 6.7%, oxygen 53.3%
6. copper 39.8%, sulphur 20.1%, oxygen 40.1%
7. calcium 40%, carbon 12%. oxygen 48%
8. silicon 46.7%, oxygen 53.3%
9. nitrogen 35%, hydrogen 5%, oxygen 60%
10. magnesium 20.3%, sulphur 26.6%, oxygen 53.1%

Chemical tests

1. B
2. A
3. E
4. F
5. C
6. E
7. B
8. A
9. D
10. B
11. C, D
12. B
13. D
14. D,(A)
15. B
16. A, B
17. C

Types of reactions 1

#		#	
1.	A	21.	A
2.	B	22.	B
3.	B	23.	B
4.	A	24.	A
5.	B	25.	B
6.	A	26.	A
7.	A	27.	A
8.	A	28.	B
9.	B	29.	B
10.	B	30.	A
11.	A	31.	B
12.	B	32.	B
13.	A	33.	A
14.	B	34.	B
15.	A	35.	A
16.	B	36.	A
17.	B	37.	A
18.	B	38.	B
19.	A	39.	B
20.	A	40.	B

Types of reactions 2

#		#	
1.	B, M	19.	D
2.	A	20.	E, L
3.	E, L	21.	H
4.	F	22.	A, J
5.	K	23.	E, L
6.	C, J	24.	C, J
7.	D	25.	A
8.	I	26.	H
9.	H	27.	F
10.	A, J	28.	I
11.	E, L	29.	H
12.	H	30.	B
13.	B, L	31.	A
14.	G	32.	H
15.	K	33.	K
16.	A	34.	H
17.	B, M	35.	E, L
18.	L		

Problem solving 1

#	
1.	D
2.	C
3.	A
4.	C
5.	C
6.	B
7.	C
8.	A
9.	A
10.	B
11.	A
12.	A
13.	B
14.	B
15.	A
16.	B
17.	A
18.	C
19.	B
20.	A
21.	C
22.	C
23.	B
24.	C
25.	A

Problem solving 2

#	
1.	A, E
2.	B, F
3.	A, D
4.	B, E
5.	E, F
6.	A, B
7.	C, D
8.	B, C
9.	A, D
10.	A, F
11.	B, D
12.	D, F
13.	A, D
14.	B, E
15.	A, F
16.	C
17.	B
18.	A

Problem solving 3

#	
1.	B
2.	E
3.	A
4.	D
5.	B
6.	D
7.	D
8.	FCADEB
9.	ECBDAF
10.	EBAFCD or BEAFCD
11.	A
12.	E

Problem solving 4

#	
1.	E
2.	B, E
3.	A
4.	B
5.	B
6.	C
7.	C
8.	B
9.	A
10.	B
11.	A
12.	C
13.	B
14.	C
15.	A
16.	B
17.	A
18.	B
19.	B
20.	A
21.	A
22.	B
23.	A
24.	B

Problem solving 5

#		#	
1.	A	23.	C
2.	A	24.	A
3.	A	25.	B
4.	B	26.	A
5.	B	27.	A
6.	A	28.	A
7.	A	29.	B
8.	B	30.	A
9.	B	31.	B
10.	A	32.	B
11.	A	33.	B
12.	A	34.	C
13.	B	35.	A
14.	B	36.	C
15.	B	37.	B
16.	B	38.	C
17.	B	39.	A
18.	A	40.	C
19.	B	41.	B
20.	B	42.	C
21.	C	43.	B
22.	A	44.	C

Problem solving 6

#		#	
1.	C	24.	B
2.	B	25.	A
3.	A, B	26.	B
4.	B, E	27.	A
5.	A, C	28.	A
6.	A	29.	B
7.	B	30.	D
8.	D, E	31.	B
9.	F	32.	A
10.	E	33.	A
11.	E	34.	A
12.	D	35.	B
13.	A	36.	B
14.	B, D	37.	A
15.	A	38.	C
16.	C	39.	C, E
17.	C	40.	D
18.	A	41.	B
19.	B	42.	B
20.	B, D	43.	A
21.	C	44.	A
22.	A	45.	B
23.	B		

1.	A	26.	D, F	51.	A	76.	A	101.	B
2.	A	27.	A	52.	B	77.	B	102.	B
3.	B	28.	B	53.	B	78.	A	103.	B
4.	A	29.	B	54.	C, D	79.	B	104.	A
5.	B	30.	B	55.	B, E	80.	A	105.	A
6.	A	31.	A	56.	A	81.	A	106.	B
7.	A	32.	A	57.	B	82.	B	107.	A
8.	A	33.	B, D	58.	B	83.	A	108.	A
9.	B	34.	B	59.	B	84.	B	109.	B
10.	A	35.	B	60.	B	85.	A	110.	B
11.	B	36.	C	61.	A	86.	B	111.	A
12.	B	37.	D	62.	B	87.	A	112.	B
13.	A	38.	D	63.	A	88.	A	113.	A
14.	A	39.	C	64.	B	89.	C	114.	B
15.	B	40.	A, B	65.	B	90.	D	115.	A
16.	A	41.	A	66.	B	91.	C	116.	B
17.	A	42.	A	67.	B	92.	A, F	117.	B
18.	B	43.	B	68.	B	93.	A	118.	A
19.	A	44.	B	69.	A	94.	B, C	118.	B
20.	B	45.	A	70.	B	95.	A, D	120.	B
21.	B	46.	A, B	71.	A	96.	A, D	121.	A
22.	A	47.	E	72.	B	97.	A	122.	B
23.	B	48.	B	73.	B	97.	A		
24.	A	49.	A	74.	B	99.	B		
25.	E	50.	B	75.	B	100.	A		